# DK BIG BOOK OF TRANSPORTATION

DK Publishing, Inc.

LONDON, NEW YORK, MUNICH,
MELBOURNE, and DELHI

**Authors** Caroline Bingham and Trevor Lord
**Publishing Manager** Sue Leonard
**Editor** Carrie Love
**U.S. Editor** John Searcy
**Production** Lucy Baker
**DTP Designer** Almudena Díaz
**Photography** Mike Dunning and Richard Leeney
**Jacket Design** Christopher Branfield
**Jacket Editor** Mariza O'Keeffe
**National Railway** Christine Heap, Stephen Hoadley,
**Museum Consultants** David Mosley

This book contains material previously published in the following DK titles:
*The Big Book of Airplanes*, 2001
*The Big Book of Cars*, 1999
*The Big Book of Race Cars*, 2001
*The Big Book of Rescue Vehicles*, 2000
*The Big Book of Trains*, 1998
*The Big Book of Trucks*, 1999

This edition published in the United States in 2006
by DK Publishing, Inc.
375 Hudson Street, New York, New York 10014

06 07 08 09 10 10 9 8 7 6 5 4 3 2 1
© 1998, 1999, 2000, 2001, 2006 Dorling Kindersley Limited

A catalog record for this book is available from the Library of Congress
ISBN 0-7566-1934-3

Color reproduction by Colourscan, Singapore
Printed and bound in Singapore by Tien Wah Press

The publisher would like to thank the following for their kind permission to
reproduce their photographs:

a = above; c = center; b = below/bottom; l = left; r = right; t = top.

Niels Jansen: 2 (logging truck), 4tl; Mercedes Benz (United Kingdom) Ltd:
5; Alvey & Towers: 6 cl, 6-7; Science Museum: 7 tr; Robert Harding Picture
Library: 12 tl; N.A.S.A.: 16 tl, 17 cr; Shaun C Connors: 22-23; Telegraph
Colour Library: Bildagentur 24 cl; Swedish State Railways:
Industrifotografen AB 24-25; Alvey & Towers: 25 tr; Alvey & Towers: 26;
South American Pictures: Tony Morrison 26 t; Photo Affairs Bildarchiv:
Jürgen Bögelspacher 26 b; Anthony J. Lambert: 27; DaimlerChrysler,
Stuttgart: 30-31 c, 30 tl, 31 tl; Brian Jennison: 30 bl, 31 tr;
Jim Winkley: 30-31; Neil Bruce/Peter Roberts Collection: Neil Bruce 31t;
Hulton Getty: 30tl; Beaulieu: 30-31c; Sylvia Cordaiy Photo Library: Geoffrey
Taunton 31 tl; Indianapolis Motor Speedway 1998 Copyright Indianapolis:
31c; Plane Picture Company: John M. Dibbs 34 c, 35 t; E.J. Koningsveld:
34 tl, 34-35; Neill Bruce: 36 t; Niels Jansen: 40 tl & 40-41; Western Truck
Company: 41 tr; Trh Pictures: 42-43 t; All-Sport: 47 cr; N.A.S.A.: 48 tl;
George Hall: 51 tr; D. & J. Heaton 56 tr; Brian Lovell 56-57; Central Japan
Railway Company: 57 tr; Impact Photos: Philip Gordon 57 br; Donald
Browning: 60 tl; Double Red 62 tl; Edwards Airforce Base/Tom Reynolds:
68 bl; Crown Copyright Sect: 73 tr; Air Tractor inc: 75 b; Velocity Inc: 83 br;
Rex Features: 88 tl; Jeremy Davey: 88 c, b, 89 c; Columbia Helicopters: 90 tl.

Discover more at
www.dk.com

Take a journey through this amazing *Big Book of Transportation* and learn about vehicles that are large and small, fast and slow, old and new. Hurry up—let's get moving!

# Contents

# CART

Drivers racing this close together next to a concrete wall need great skill and a lot of courage.

CART (Championship Auto Racing Teams) was set up in the US to organize races on street circuits, racetracks, and banked ovals. The same cars and drivers race at all three types of track, so the drivers have to be more versatile than those racing in Formula One. The season, which lasts 10 months, takes the teams all around the world.

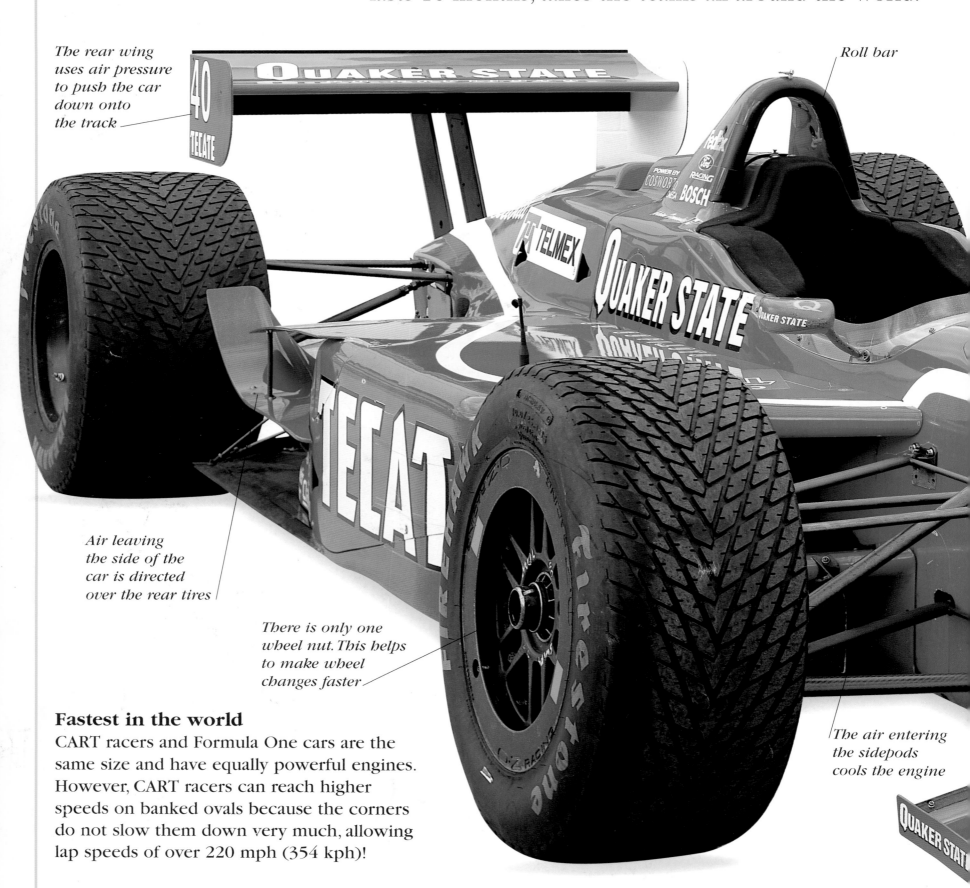

The rear wing uses air pressure to push the car down onto the track

Roll bar

Air leaving the side of the car is directed over the rear tires

There is only one wheel nut. This helps to make wheel changes faster

The air entering the sidepods cools the engine

## Fastest in the world

CART racers and Formula One cars are the same size and have equally powerful engines. However, CART racers can reach higher speeds on banked ovals because the corners do not slow them down very much, allowing lap speeds of over 220 mph (354 kph)!

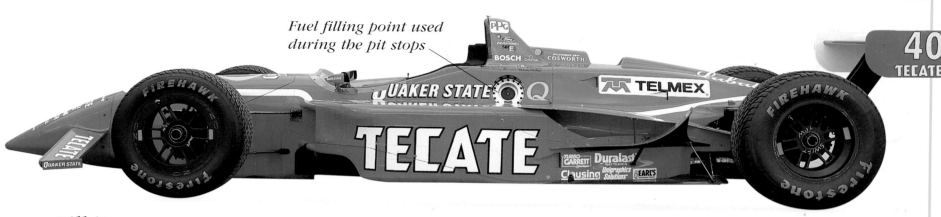

Fuel filling point used during the pit stops

## Fill it up

With a fuel tank capacity of 41 gallons (159 liters), this car can only race for about 130 miles (207 kilometers). To continue the race, the driver has to make a pit stop and refuel.

## Ready for rain

These tires have tread. They are used when the car is raced on a wet track and are called "wets." The tires used on a dry track are completely smooth, and they are known as "slicks."

The mirror allows the driver to watch the cars behind

This panel can be removed to adjust the suspension

This rod is moved by the steering wheel to help steer the car

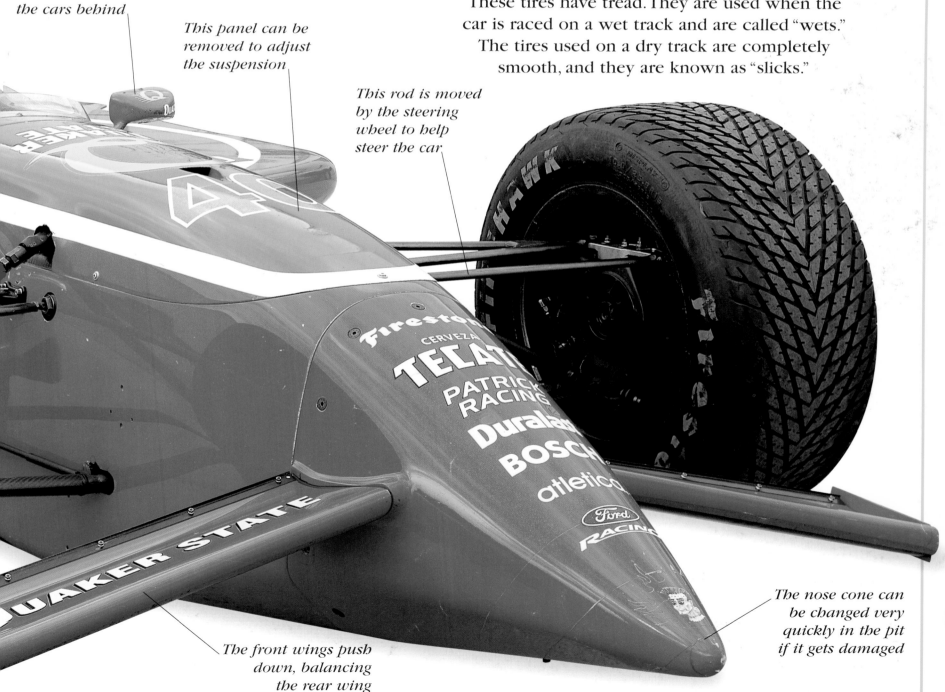

The nose cone can be changed very quickly in the pit if it gets damaged

The front wings push down, balancing the rear wing

5

# Mobile home toter

This house is being moved by a specially adapted truck called a mobile home toter. This short truck can haul a house over three times its own length. The house is towed complete with wallpaper, carpets, and curtains.

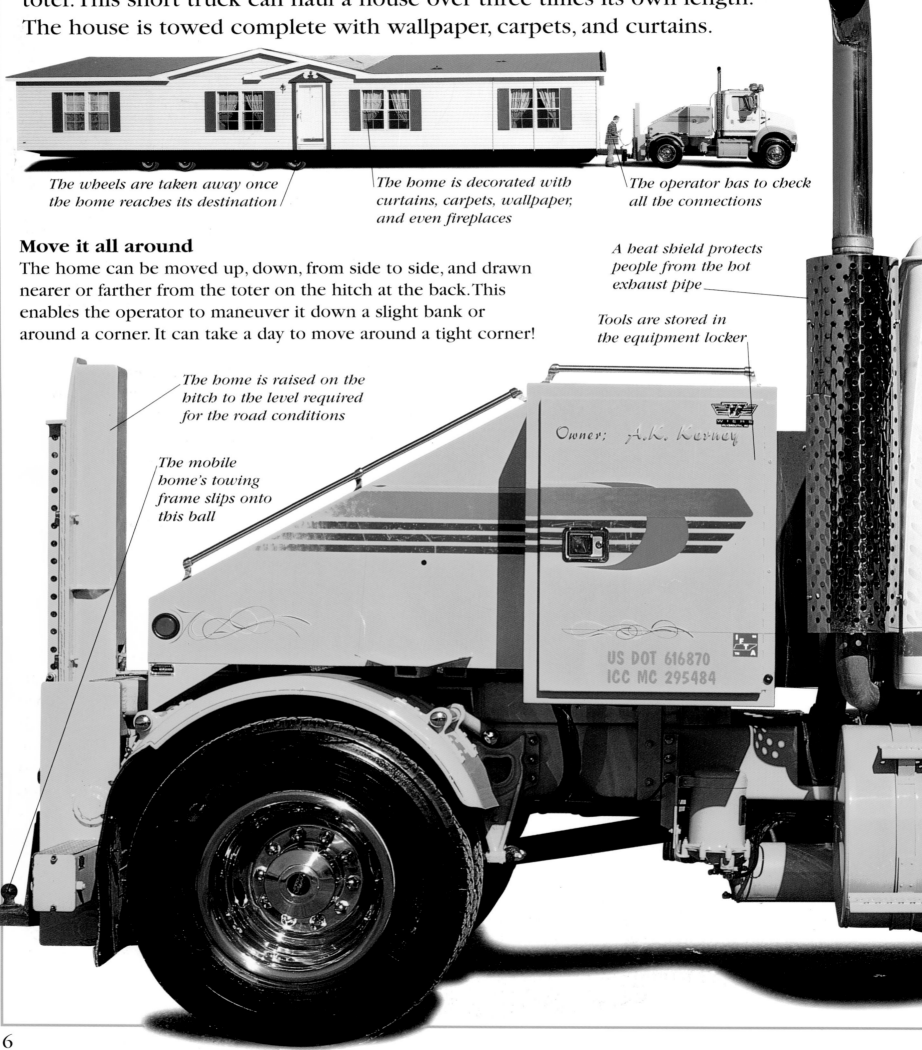

The wheels are taken away once the home reaches its destination

The home is decorated with curtains, carpets, wallpaper, and even fireplaces

The operator has to check all the connections

## Move it all around

The home can be moved up, down, from side to side, and drawn nearer or farther from the toter on the hitch at the back. This enables the operator to maneuver it down a slight bank or around a corner. It can take a day to move around a tight corner!

A heat shield protects people from the hot exhaust pipe

Tools are stored in the equipment locker

The home is raised on the hitch to the level required for the road conditions

The mobile home's towing frame slips onto this ball

Owner: A.K. Kerney

US DOT 616870
ICC MC 295484

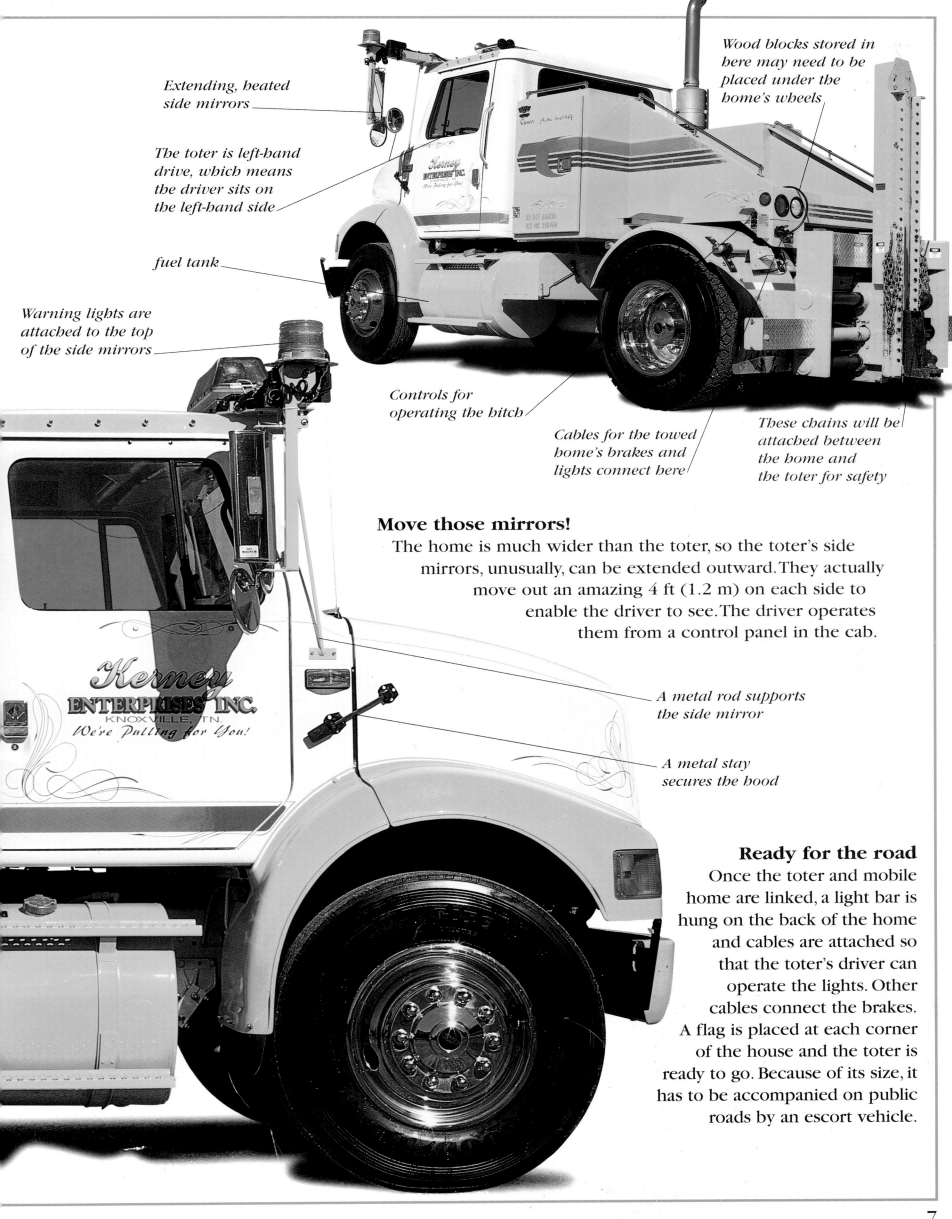

Extending, heated side mirrors

The toter is left-hand drive, which means the driver sits on the left-hand side

fuel tank

Warning lights are attached to the top of the side mirrors

Wood blocks stored in here may need to be placed under the home's wheels

Controls for operating the hitch

Cables for the towed home's brakes and lights connect here

These chains will be attached between the home and the toter for safety

Kerney ENTERPRISES INC. KNOXVILLE, TN. We're Putting for You!

## Move those mirrors!

The home is much wider than the toter, so the toter's side mirrors, unusually, can be extended outward. They actually move out an amazing 4 ft (1.2 m) on each side to enable the driver to see. The driver operates them from a control panel in the cab.

A metal rod supports the side mirror

A metal stay secures the hood

## Ready for the road

Once the toter and mobile home are linked, a light bar is hung on the back of the home and cables are attached so that the toter's driver can operate the lights. Other cables connect the brakes. A flag is placed at each corner of the house and the toter is ready to go. Because of its size, it has to be accompanied on public roads by an escort vehicle.

# Heavy rescue truck

Some emergencies require extra help, and this amazing fire truck can provide just that. It is packed with equipment to help rescuers tackle different problems at rescue sites. It also has a huge crane that can be used to raise and lower people and equipment to exactly where needed.

**It's in the locker!**
The heavy rescue truck carries more than 100 pieces of equipment, including cutters capable of cutting metal, and water rescue gear.

Crane

Harnesses

*The orange sacks contain ropes*

*These huge cutters will open up a car in minutes*

ABERDEEN FIRE DEPT.

*These air bags can be inflated to lift a heavy object*

*Air bottles*

*The bus-style mirrors have two parts. One gives vision close up, the other further back*

HEAVY RESCUE

Siren

*The front bumper contains a winch*

ABERDEEN

ABERDEEN
SINCE
251
1889
FIRE DEPT.

*Two lockers in the front bumper hold chains for use with the winch*

*Air horn*

*Chocks prevent the truck from moving when the crane is in use*

## Winch it up

The boom extends 50 feet (15 meters) and is used to recover a car from a ditch or to stabilize a vehicle that has rolled. It is also used to lift a metal box called a trench pod off the truck and into areas where it may be required. This box contains panels and beams that are used to stabilize walls in a confined space that may otherwise collapse.

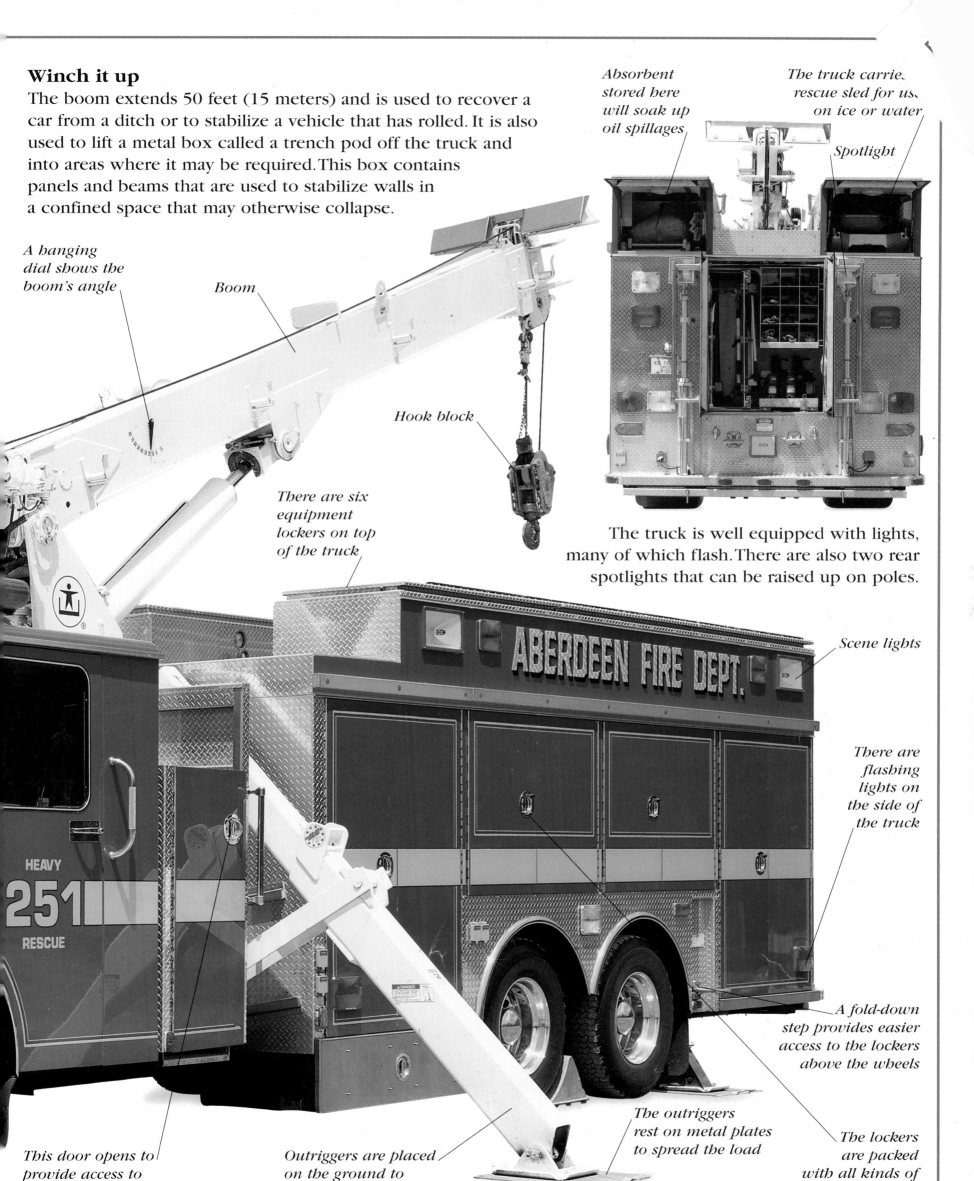

*A hanging dial shows the boom's angle*

*Boom*

*Hook block*

*There are six equipment lockers on top of the truck*

*Absorbent stored here will soak up oil spillages*

*The truck carries rescue sled for use on ice or water*

*Spotlight*

The truck is well equipped with lights, many of which flash. There are also two rear spotlights that can be raised up on poles.

*Scene lights*

*There are flashing lights on the side of the truck*

**ABERDEEN FIRE DEPT.**

HEAVY

251

RESCUE

*This door opens to provide access to controls for the crane*

*Outriggers are placed on the ground to keep the truck steady*

*The outriggers rest on metal plates to spread the load*

*A fold-down step provides easier access to the lockers above the wheels*

*The lockers are packed with all kinds of vital equipment*

# Dragster

In drag races, two cars race against each other in a straight line over a distance of 1,300 feet (400 meters). The cars are more powerful than those used in any other type of motor sport. Drag racing started in the US, but it is now popular all around the world.

### Funny car!

"Funny cars" are dragsters that have lightweight bodies built to look like a standard production car. Of all the dragster classes equipped with full bodies, funny cars are the fastest and most spectacular.

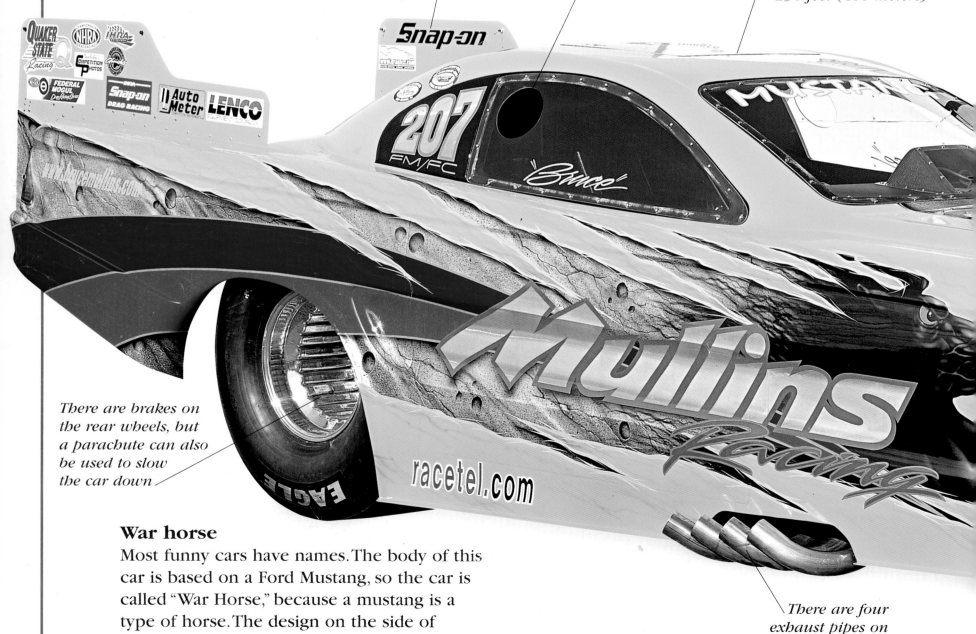

*The fins help to keep the dragster traveling in a straight line*

*The windows do not open, so these holes let in fresh air for the driver*

*This car uses 1,500 times as much fuel as a family car would need to cover 250 feet (400 meters)*

*There are brakes on the rear wheels, but a parachute can also be used to slow the car down*

*There are four exhaust pipes on each side of the car*

### War horse

Most funny cars have names. The body of this car is based on a Ford Mustang, so the car is called "War Horse," because a mustang is a type of horse. The design on the side of the car reflects the car's name.

*This engine will take the car to 236 mph (380 kph) in less than 6 seconds!*

*For safety reasons, the fuel tank is positioned as far away from the driver as possible*

*The supercharger pushes air into the engine to make it more powerful*

*An onboard fire extinguisher is attached in case of fire*

## Nose in the air

The body of a funny car can be lifted clear of the engine, making it easier for the mechanics to work on the car. This is very important because the powerful engine has to be rebuilt with new parts after each race.

*Air intakes*

There are no doors on a dragster, so the driver has to be seated and strapped in before the body is lowered.

*The front wheels will lift clear of the ground at the start of a run*

# Road train

Train locomotives are capable of hauling 12 or more carriages, but most trucks are restricted to hauling one or two trailers. Road trains are named because, although they are trucks, they can haul three or four trailers. They are commonly used in Australia, where the distances between cities are huge.

## Head on
A road train's tractor or 'prime mover' can be 30 ft (9 m) long and weigh the same as 9 family cars.

## Built for distance
The fuel tanks can hold 530 gallons (2000 liters); about 30 times the amount of a family car. This capacity is required so that the truck doesn't have to keep stopping to refuel on a journey of, perhaps, 2000 miles (3500 km). However, the driver does have to take breaks!

*The trailers bend where they link together*

*One end of each trailer is supported by the axles of the trailer in front*

*These trailers have four axles each*

*The first trailer connects to a fitting called the fifth wheel*

There are cab-over road trains as well as conventional ones.

## No entry!
Road trains are not as long as trains, but they are big compared to other road vehicles. The maximum allowed length is 165 ft (50 m), so they are too long to negotiate city streets, and must stop at special road train unloading stations.

Flashing lights warn other road users of a long load

The exhaust pipes tower 14 ft (4.2 m) above the road

Air is sucked in through these pipes to be filtered. It mixes with the fuel to make the engine run

Side mirrors extending from the cab give the driver good rear vision

The hood lifts forward to provide access to the engine

Bull bar

MACK

Mack

Mack

# Mountain trains

Railroads are very popular in mountainous areas where it would be difficult to build a road. Many mountain railroads were built just so that people could enjoy the view from the train. Rack railroads have special tracks that can run up the sides of mountains. The train has a powered cogwheel under the engine, which grips a toothed rail. This allows the train to climb very steep slopes and prevents it from slipping backward.

**World's highest railroad**
The Huancayo-Huancay line in Peru is the world's highest railroad. This ordinary railroad reaches a height of 15,846 feet (4,830 meters). The steam locomotives that run here were built in England.

**Tourist train**
The Brienz Rothorn train is now just a tourist attraction. This rack railroad is 5 miles (7.5 kilometers) long and is the only one in Switzerland that still uses steam locomotives. Powerful engines push the passenger cars up the mountainside, to a height of 5,511 feet (1,680 meters).

*The passenger car is pushed uphill by the steam locomotive.*

*A cogged wheel on the engine climbs up the toothed rack.*

*The locomotive is built at an angle so that it stays level on the steep slope.*

**Bridges and tunnels**
Railroads in mountainous areas have to use many bridges, viaducts, and tunnels to pass through difficult terrain. This train is called the *Glacier Express* because it runs through deep snow for many months of the year. It carries passengers to ski resorts in the Swiss mountains.

## Steepest rack railroad

The Mount Pilatus Railroad in Switzerland is the steepest rack railroad in the world. The railroad used steam engines when it was opened in 1889, but electric trains took over in 1937. The trains are single cars and have a top speed of 6 miles (9 kilometers) per hour.

*The pantograph collects electricity from the wires running overhead.*

*The cars are specially designed so that the passenger seats match the angle of the slope.*

*Some sections of the track slide sideways to enable trains to pass each other.*

*Trains travel up and down the mountain on the same track.*

*The rack is laid between the ordinary rails.*

# Flying laboratory

This unusual looking long-nosed plane is designed to cruise at altitudes of about 13.5 miles (22 km). That's more than twice the cruising altitude of a jumbo jet! It needs to do this because it is a flying science aircraft, or flying laboratory, specially equipped to collect information about the Earth. Its official name is the ER-2.

The ER-2 has four compartments that hold experiments. One is in the fuselage, one is in the nose, and two are in pods that can be attached to the wings.

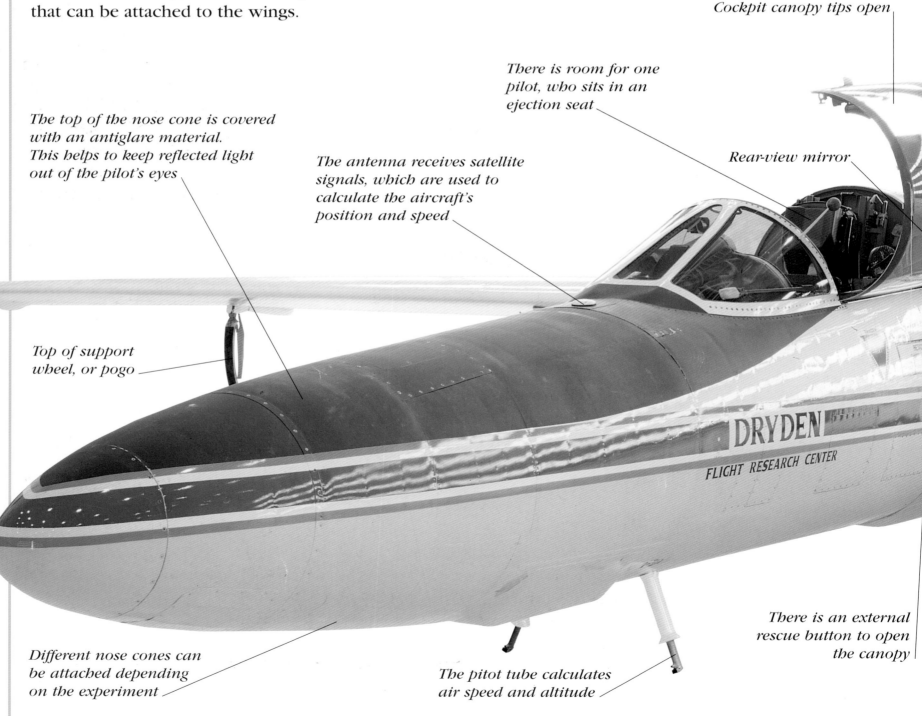

*Cockpit canopy tips open*

*There is room for one pilot, who sits in an ejection seat*

*Rear-view mirror*

*The top of the nose cone is covered with an antiglare material. This helps to keep reflected light out of the pilot's eyes*

*The antenna receives satellite signals, which are used to calculate the aircraft's position and speed*

*Top of support wheel, or pogo*

*There is an external rescue button to open the canopy*

*Different nose cones can be attached depending on the experiment*

*The pitot tube calculates air speed and altitude*

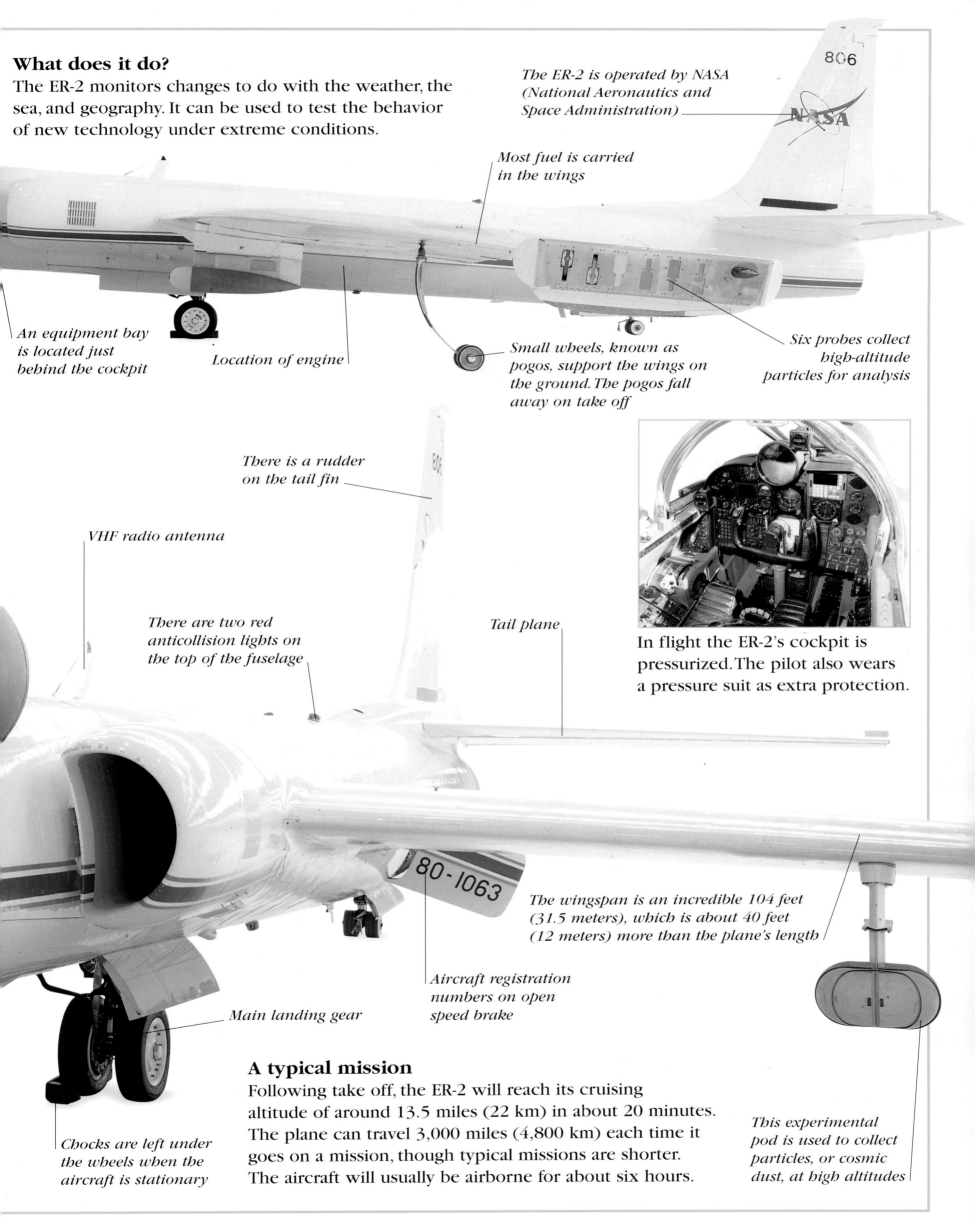

## What does it do?

The ER-2 monitors changes to do with the weather, the sea, and geography. It can be used to test the behavior of new technology under extreme conditions.

*The ER-2 is operated by NASA (National Aeronautics and Space Administration)*

*806*

*NASA*

*Most fuel is carried in the wings*

*An equipment bay is located just behind the cockpit*

*Location of engine*

*Small wheels, known as pogos, support the wings on the ground. The pogos fall away on take off*

*Six probes collect high-altitude particles for analysis*

*There is a rudder on the tail fin*

*VHF radio antenna*

*There are two red anticollision lights on the top of the fuselage*

*Tail plane*

In flight the ER-2's cockpit is pressurized. The pilot also wears a pressure suit as extra protection.

*80-1063*

*The wingspan is an incredible 104 feet (31.5 meters), which is about 40 feet (12 meters) more than the plane's length*

*Aircraft registration numbers on open speed brake*

*Main landing gear*

*Chocks are left under the wheels when the aircraft is stationary*

## A typical mission

Following take off, the ER-2 will reach its cruising altitude of around 13.5 miles (22 km) in about 20 minutes. The plane can travel 3,000 miles (4,800 km) each time it goes on a mission, though typical missions are shorter. The aircraft will usually be airborne for about six hours.

*This experimental pod is used to collect particles, or cosmic dust, at high altitudes*

# Classic race cars

The early race cars first competed in city-to-city races.

The idea of using cars for races is not a new one. In fact, cars were first used for races before they were ever used for personal transport. Since those early days, motor races have not only provided exciting entertainment, but have helped to make the cars we use on the road today both safer and faster by developing new ideas on the racetrack. Disc brakes, aluminum wheels, and rear-view mirrors were all first used on race cars.

*Rear-view mirror*

*The yellow and black color scheme gave this car the name "Wasp"*

*This pointed tail is an early attempt at streamlining*

*Even in 1911 pit stops were used to change tires*

*The Type 35 was a two-seater race car*

*The Bugatti Type 35 won the very first Monaco Grand Prix*

*The gear lever, like the handbrake, was placed outside so that the car could be as narrow as possible*

*Handbrake*

**Marmon Wasp**

The Marmon Wasp won the first Indianapolis 500 race in 1911. The car is also famous for being probably the first car in the world to be fitted with a rear-view mirror.

**Bugatti Type 35**

The Bugatti Type 35 is one of the most successful cars in the history of motor races. Around 400 were built, and between them they won nearly 2,000 races in the period 1924 to 1931! Many people have also described it as the most beautiful race car ever made. It was also the first car in the world to be fitted with aluminum wheels.

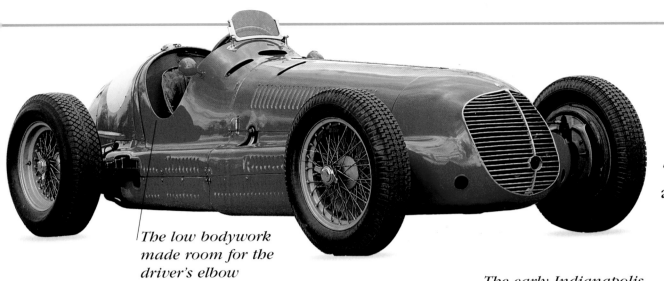

*The low bodywork made room for the driver's elbow*

## Maserati Tipo 8CTF

This 1938 Tipo was built to race in Grands Prix. It did not win any, but instead won the Indianapolis 500 in 1939. The Maseratis, like the Ferraris and Alfa Romeos, were painted red—the racing color of Italy.

*The early Indianapolis cars did not have sponsorship stickers*

## Kurtis-Offenhauser

Cars like this Kurtis-Offenhauser raced on the banked, oval tracks of the United States. But the cars regularly scored points in the World Drivers' Championship in the 1950s. This was because the Indianapolis 500 was included in the championship at that time.

*The strap stopped the hood from flying open during the race*

*The grille protected the radiator from stones*

*The starting handle was used to start the engine*

*This arm is connected to the steering wheel and operates the steering*

*Aluminum wheels*

# Snow trains

When railroad tracks become blocked by snow, special trains are needed to dig out the tracks so that trains can start running again. Snowplows can be used to clear deep snowdrifts, but in really severe conditions, rotary snowblowers are needed to open up the tracks. These snow trains were first used in the United States in 1869.

*Loose snow was broken up by the wheel, blown out of this chute, and thrown clear of the track.*

*The powerful headlight could light up the track in blizzard conditions.*

*Large side blades sliced a path through the snowdrifts and channeled the snow into the spinning wheel.*

*The giant spinning wheel broke up the snow.*

*The snowblower was powered by steam from a boiler inside the blower.*

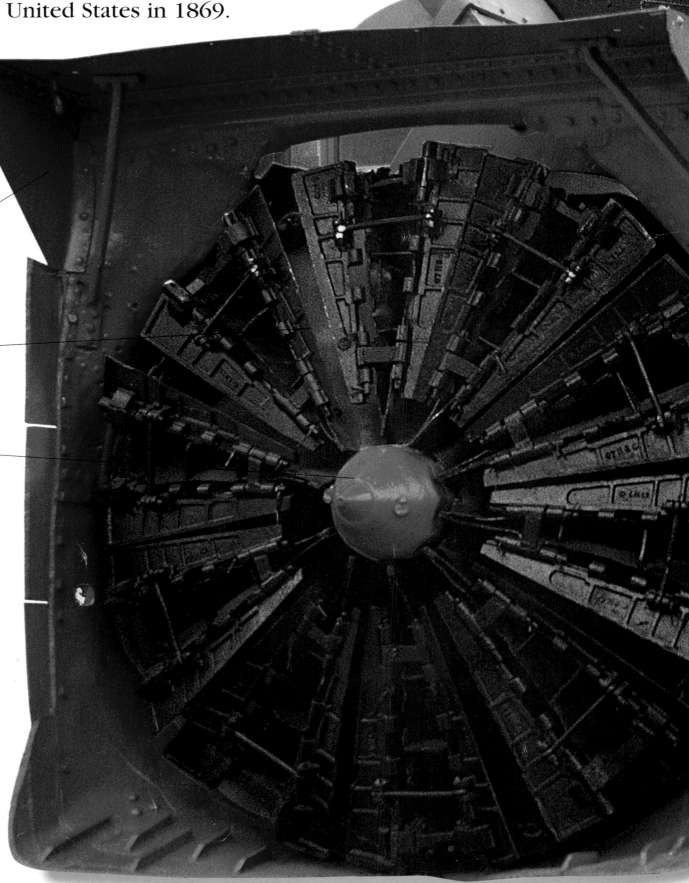

**Clearing tracks**
Snowblowers clear the tracks before other trains start running. In very heavy snow storms, they may be needed to rescue stranded trains.

## Diesel power

This British snow train is diesel-powered and does not need a locomotive to push it. Large blades break up the snow, which is then blown clear of the track. Deep snow is rare in Britain, so the train is stored in a depot when not in use.

## Snowblower at work

This steam-powered snowblower clears the tracks by cutting into the snowdrift and then blowing the loose snow away from the tracks. The train can clear about 131 feet (40 meters) of deep snow per minute and is moved along the tracks by "pusher" locomotives.

*The tender carried the coal and water to fuel the boiler.*

*This vehicle contained equipment and facilities for the crew.*

## Steam snowblower

This snowblower worked on the railroads of Alaska, and was powered by steam. It had a crew of three: the fireman, the engineer who took care of the machinery, and the pilot who signaled to the "pusher" locomotives.

# Amphibious truck

You won't see many trucks that look like this. This amazing truck can drive off a road and into a lake or river. Its top then flips open to turn it into a floating bridge. It can also connect with others like it to form either bridges or ferries for transporting people and vehicles.

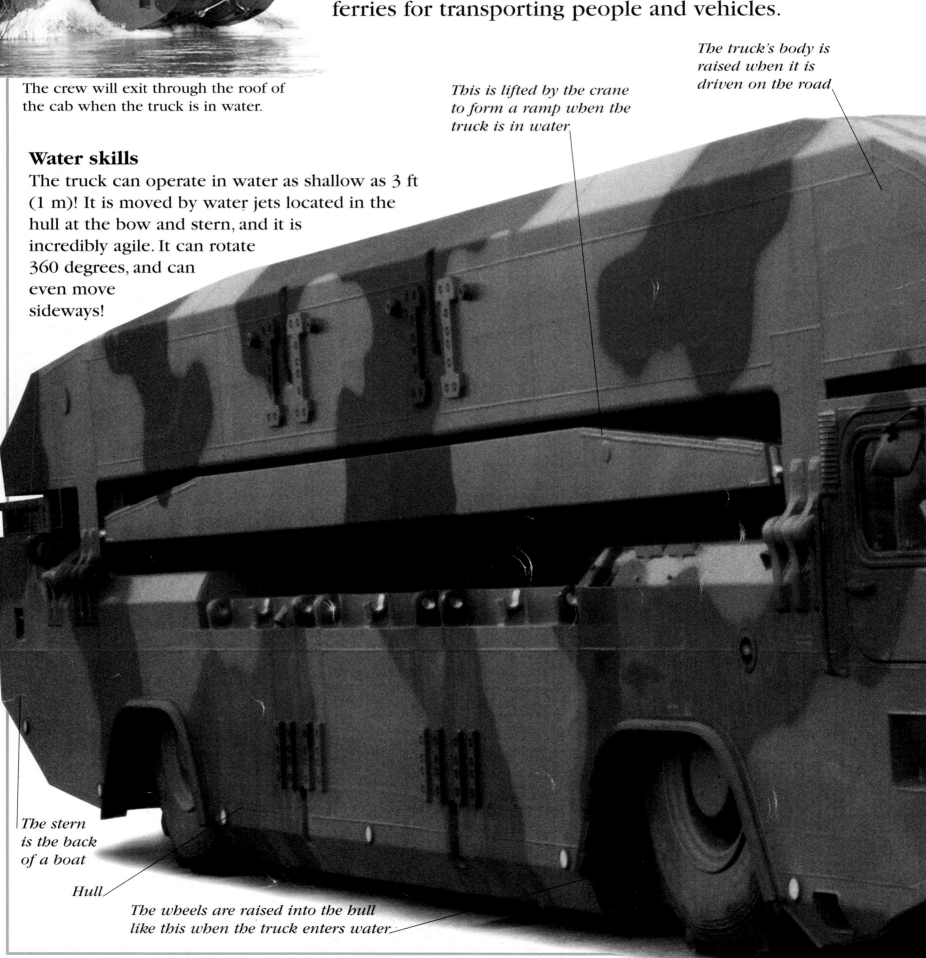

The crew will exit through the roof of the cab when the truck is in water.

*This is lifted by the crane to form a ramp when the truck is in water*

*The truck's body is raised when it is driven on the road*

## Water skills

The truck can operate in water as shallow as 3 ft (1 m)! It is moved by water jets located in the hull at the bow and stern, and it is incredibly agile. It can rotate 360 degrees, and can even move sideways!

*The stern is the back of a boat*

*Hull*

*The wheels are raised into the hull like this when the truck enters water.*

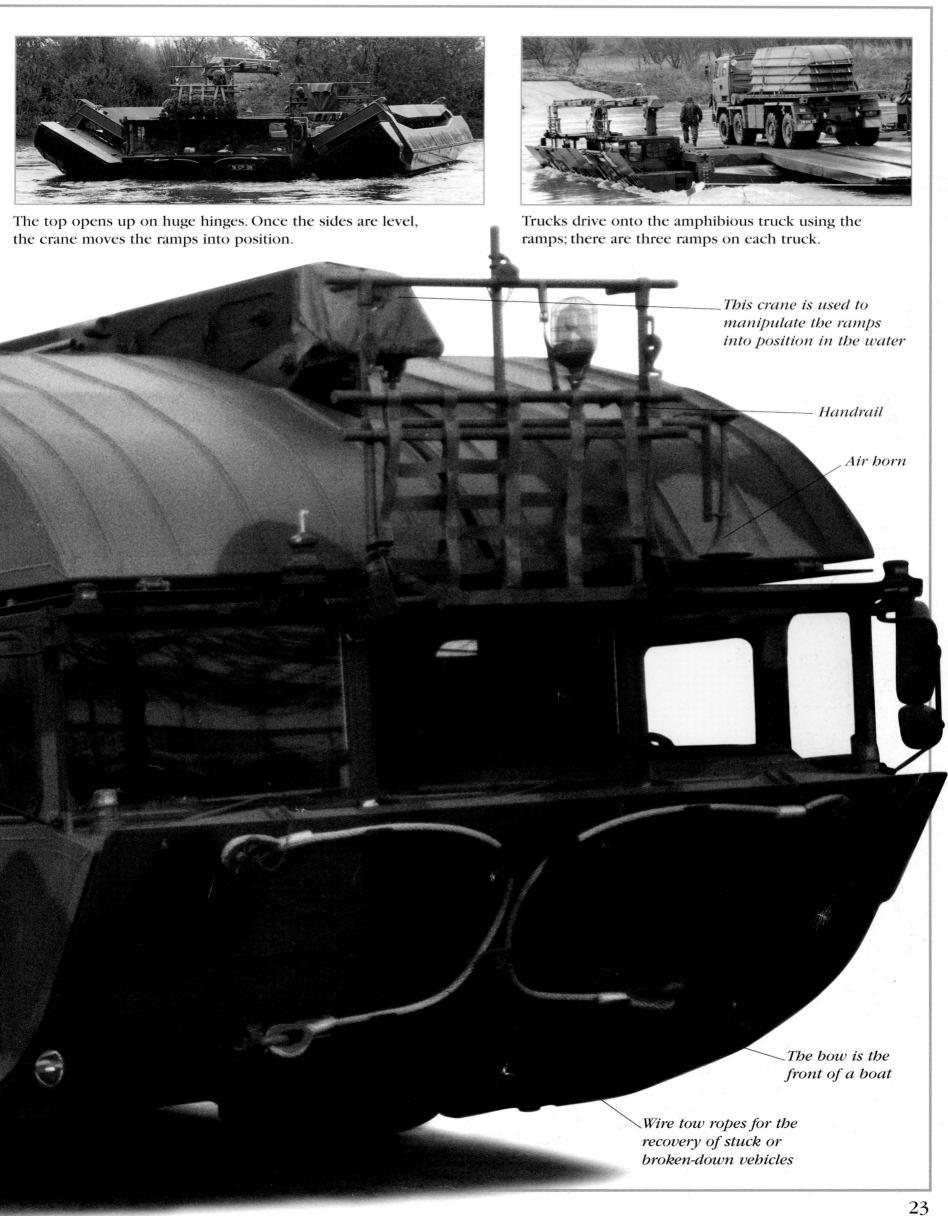

The top opens up on huge hinges. Once the sides are level, the crane moves the ramps into position.

Trucks drive onto the amphibious truck using the ramps; there are three ramps on each truck.

*This crane is used to manipulate the ramps into position in the water*

*Handrail*

*Air horn*

*The bow is the front of a boat*

*Wire tow ropes for the recovery of stuck or broken-down vehicles*

# High-speed passenger trains

Electric trains are now running at faster and faster speeds, because they have to compete with cars and airplanes for passengers traveling between major cities. High-speed passenger trains run on electric power picked up from overhead lines. Some countries have built brand-new railroad networks for their fast electric trains. Others run a high-speed service on existing tracks and fit the trains into their normal schedules.

*The train has a driving car at both ends, which makes it possible to depart right away on the return trip.*

*Headlights or taillights are used, depending on which way the train is traveling.*

**Fast and slow tracks**
Germany's high-speed trains run on both existing tracks and newly built lines. The ICE electric engines can run only at their top speed of 174 miles (280 kilometers) per hour when traveling on the new lines.

*The lip on the power car acts as a small snowplow.*

*The driving trailer has space for carrying baggage.*

**England to Scotland**
The GNER 225 has a top speed of 140 miles (225 kilometers) per hour. It runs between London and Edinburgh on Britain's Great North Eastern Railway.

## Traveling on straight lines

The new Italian ETR 500 can travel at 190 miles (300 kilometers) per hour. It runs on specially built high-speed routes with few curves. This means that the train can maintain its fast speed without slowing down for curves or other traffic on the line.

*The pantograph picks up electric power from overhead wires.*

## Tilting train

The railroads of Sweden are all twists and turns. The engine and cars of the X2000 train tilt when going around corners. This enables the train to keep up its top speed of 125 miles (200 kilometers) per hour.

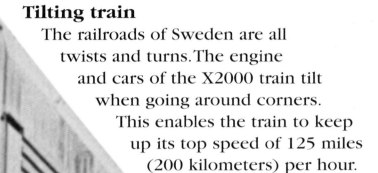

*The X2000 power car pulls five passenger cars on its intercity trips.*

# Inshore lifeboat

An inshore lifeboat is ideal for rescuing people in trouble close to shore. It might race to find a jet ski that has broken down or pick up a child whose dinghy has drifted too far out. It is faster than a larger lifeboat, and its fuel tanks can keep it going at top speed for three hours.

## All sealed up

The inshore lifeboat has a shaped plastic hull. An inflatable tube, called a sponson, runs around the top of the hull. Both the hull and the sponson are divided into watertight compartments, so if one section is damaged, the boat will still float. It is known as a rigid inflatable boat, or RIB.

The two outboard motors are waterproofed. If the boat capsizes, they will restart!

*Radio antenna*

*Flashing blue light*

*The helmsman controls the boat's speed with his right hand*

*Inflatable airbag*

*A radar reflector allows other boats to "see" the lifeboat on their radar*

*There are two fuel tanks beneath the deck*

PHYL CLARE 3

*Handgrip*

B-746

The airbag is held on a metal cradle

Inflated airbag

**Over and up**

If the lifeboat capsizes, the crew swim to the stern. There they pull on a metal ring and a gas bottle inflates a large airbag. Within seconds, the lifeboat rights itself and the boat is ready to set off again.

If someone is in the water, they can grab this lifeline

Control panel

Water is carried in the bow to keep it low when breaking through waves. Once past the breakers, the water is released

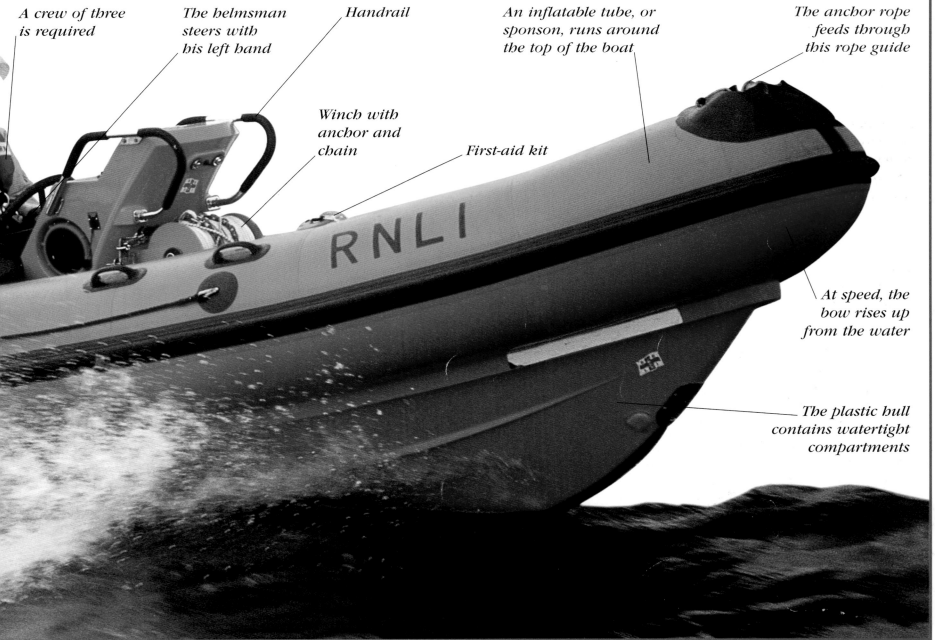

A crew of three is required

The helmsman steers with his left hand

Handrail

An inflatable tube, or sponson, runs around the top of the boat

The anchor rope feeds through this rope guide

Winch with anchor and chain

First-aid kit

At speed, the bow rises up from the water

The plastic hull contains watertight compartments

# Baja buggy

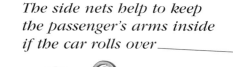

The annual Baja 1000 is one of the world's toughest motor races. The drivers have to tackle 1,000 miles (1,600 kilometers) of desert terrain at speeds of up to 120 mph (193 kph). Other vehicles, such as pickup trucks and bikes also compete. But the race is so tough that sometimes only a quarter of the starters make it to the finish.

Driving at high speed across rocks, boulders, and sand dunes often results in the cars taking off into the air.

## Baja Buggy

To finish the Baja 1000, a car must be extremely strong. The best buggies are built around a cage made of steel tubing. This cage is strong enough to survive the many bumps and bangs it will face during the race. The strong frame also gives some protection to the driver and navigator if the car crashes.

The side nets help to keep the passenger's arms inside if the car rolls over

A high ground clearance enables the buggy to drive over rocks

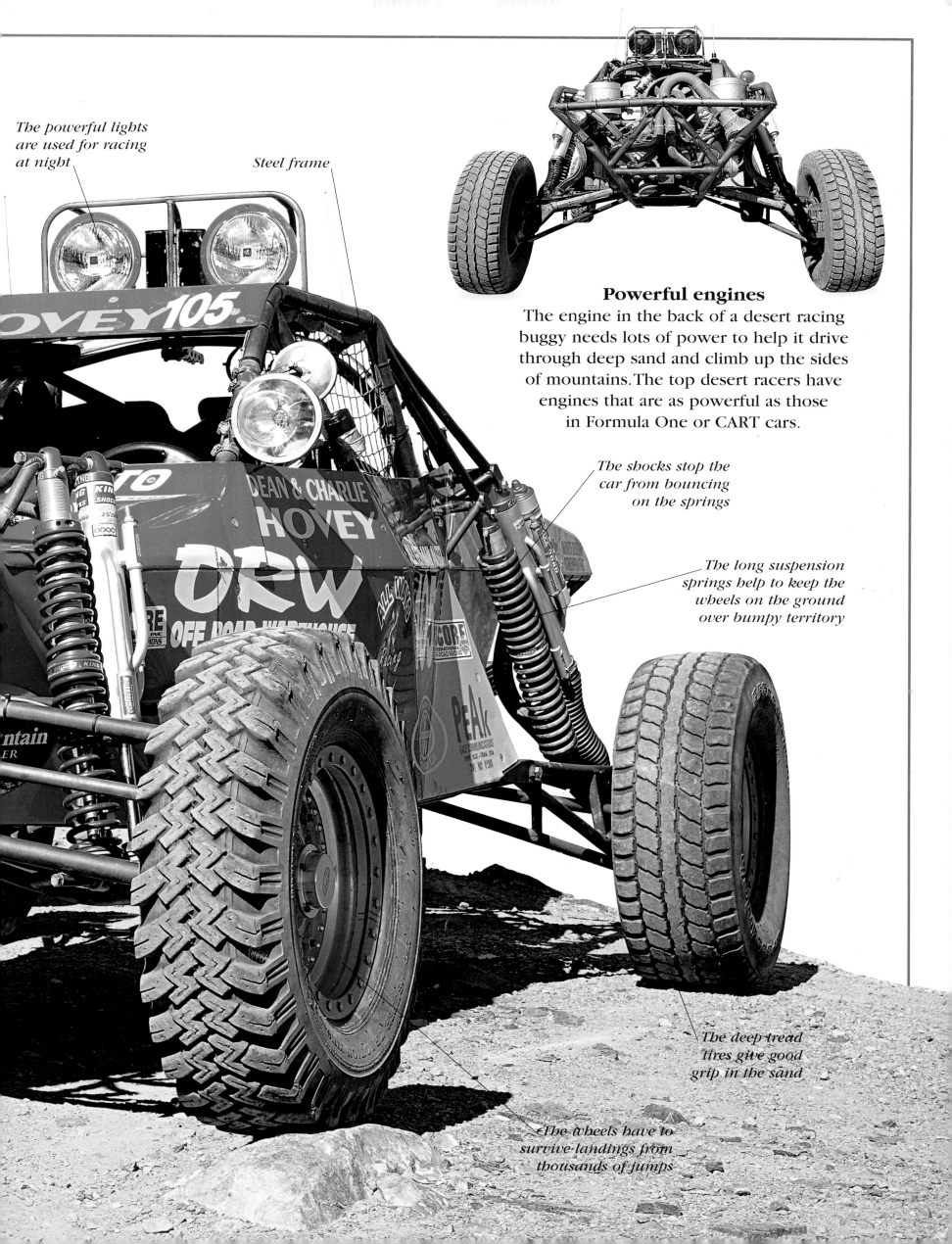

*The powerful lights are used for racing at night*

*Steel frame*

## Powerful engines

The engine in the back of a desert racing buggy needs lots of power to help it drive through deep sand and climb up the sides of mountains. The top desert racers have engines that are as powerful as those in Formula One or CART cars.

*The shocks stop the car from bouncing on the springs*

*The long suspension springs help to keep the wheels on the ground over bumpy territory*

*The deep tread tires give good grip in the sand*

*The wheels have to survive landings from thousands of jumps*

# Concept truck

Truck manufacturers sometimes build concept trucks to try out new ideas. They look at questions of safety and fuel efficiency (or how far the truck will go on a certain amount of fuel). They also consider issues such as how a truck's exhaust fumes affect the environment. The resulting trucks are usually eye-catching, and some of the ideas tested will then find their way into the design of trucks that are actually being built.

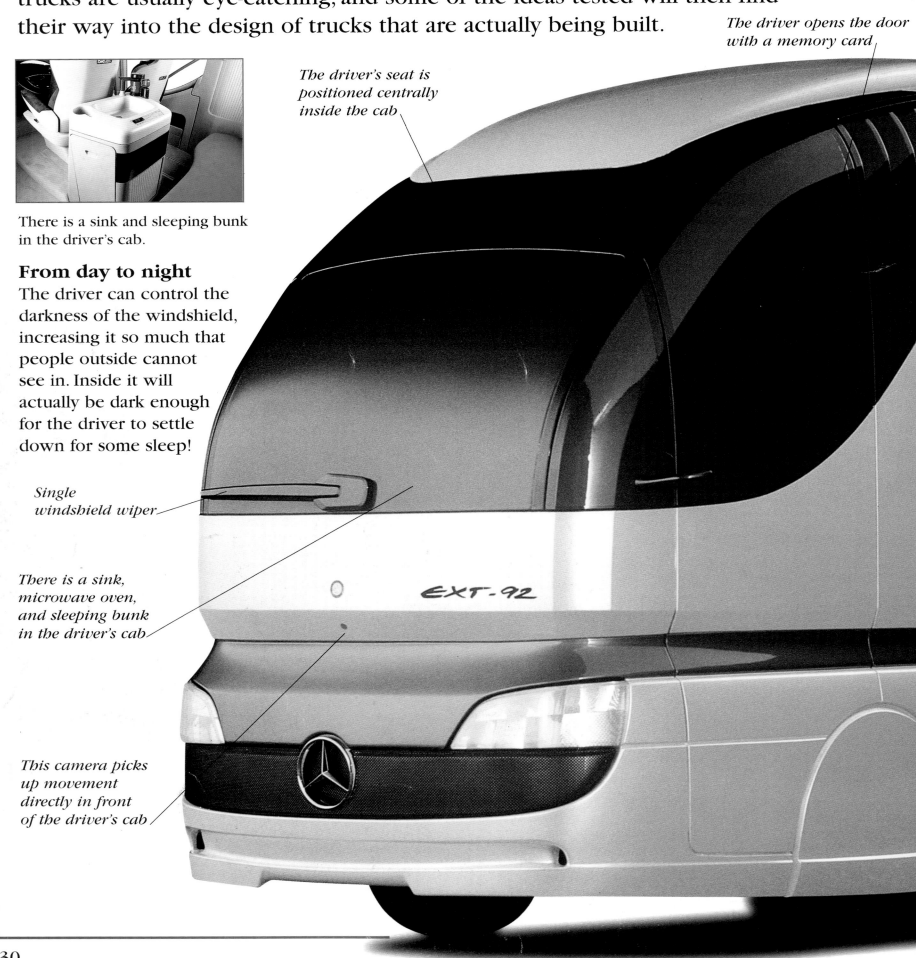

*The driver opens the door with a memory card*

*The driver's seat is positioned centrally inside the cab*

There is a sink and sleeping bunk in the driver's cab.

## From day to night

The driver can control the darkness of the windshield, increasing it so much that people outside cannot see in. Inside it will actually be dark enough for the driver to settle down for some sleep!

*Single windshield wiper*

*There is a sink, microwave oven, and sleeping bunk in the driver's cab*

EXT-92

*This camera picks up movement directly in front of the driver's cab*

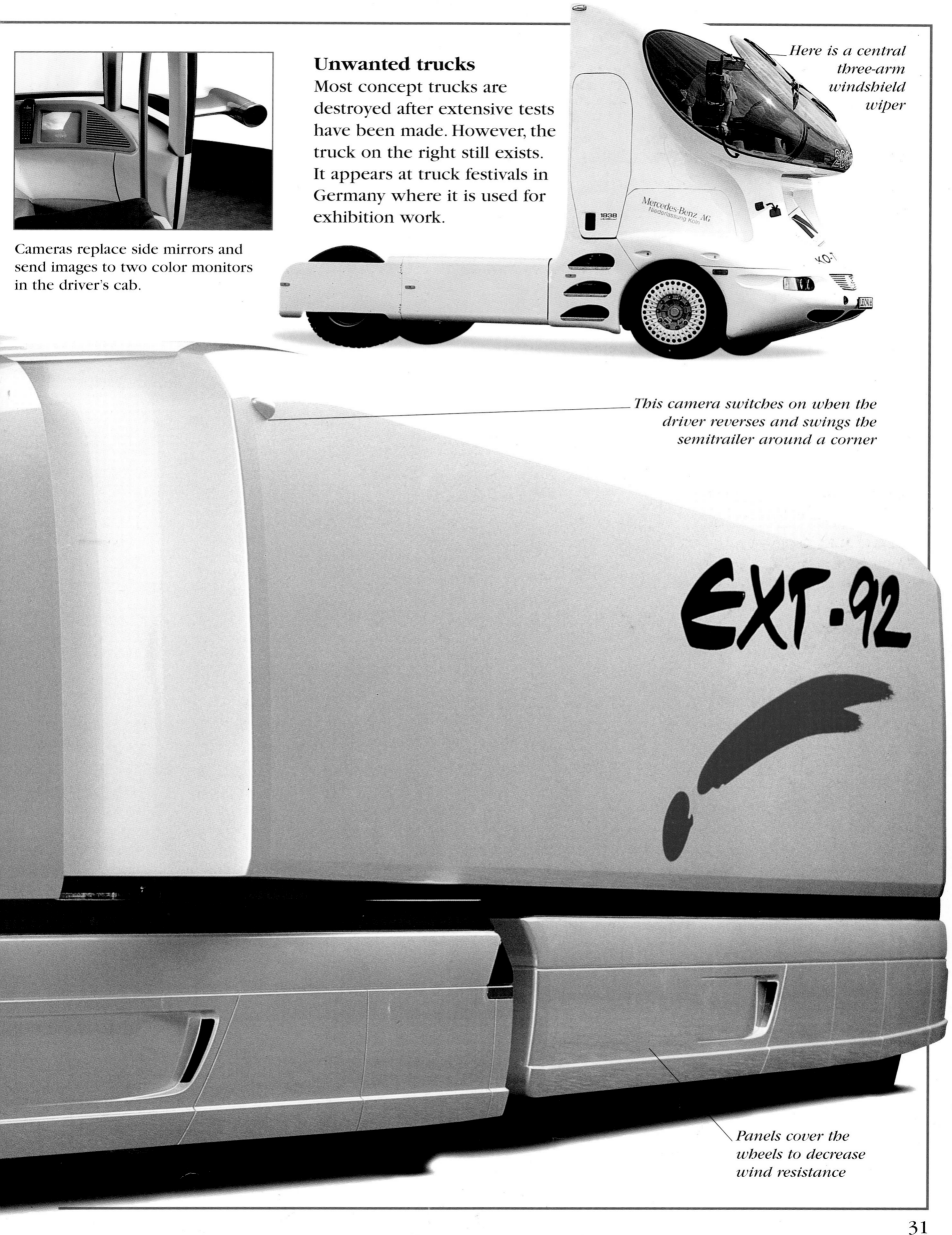

Cameras replace side mirrors and send images to two color monitors in the driver's cab.

## Unwanted trucks

Most concept trucks are destroyed after extensive tests have been made. However, the truck on the right still exists. It appears at truck festivals in Germany where it is used for exhibition work.

*Here is a central three-arm windshield wiper*

Mercedes-Benz AG
Niederlassung Köln

1838

EXT.92

*This camera switches on when the driver reverses and swings the semitrailer around a corner*

*Panels cover the wheels to decrease wind resistance*

# Airport fire truck

This fire truck carries six times more water than many of the fire engines you'll see on the road. It can also pump water at least four times faster. The truck has to be able to carry and pump more water as the incidents it is called to may not always be near a water source.

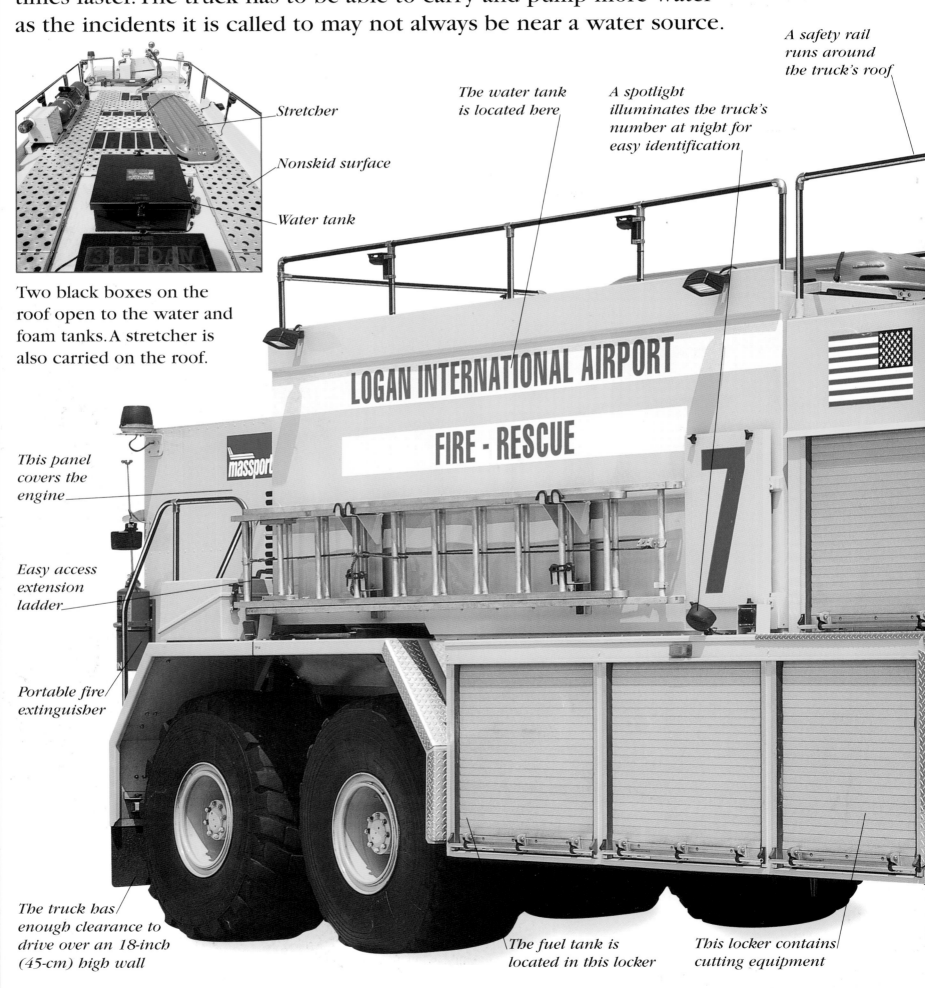

Two black boxes on the roof open to the water and foam tanks. A stretcher is also carried on the roof.

Stretcher

Nonskid surface

Water tank

*A safety rail runs around the truck's roof*

*The water tank is located here*

*A spotlight illuminates the truck's number at night for easy identification*

*This panel covers the engine*

*Easy access extension ladder*

*Portable fire extinguisher*

LOGAN INTERNATIONAL AIRPORT

FIRE - RESCUE

massport

7

*The truck has enough clearance to drive over an 18-inch (45-cm) high wall*

*The fuel tank is located in this locker*

*This locker contains cutting equipment*

# Finding and flooding a hot spot

On top of the driver's cab is a heat-seeking camera. This is linked up to a screen in the cab where the crew are able to see hot spots inside an airplane. Hot spots show up on the screen as areas of white. The firefighters can then target this area with the two nozzles at the front of the truck, controlling them with joy sticks. To fire a jet of water a firefighter simply squeezes a button.

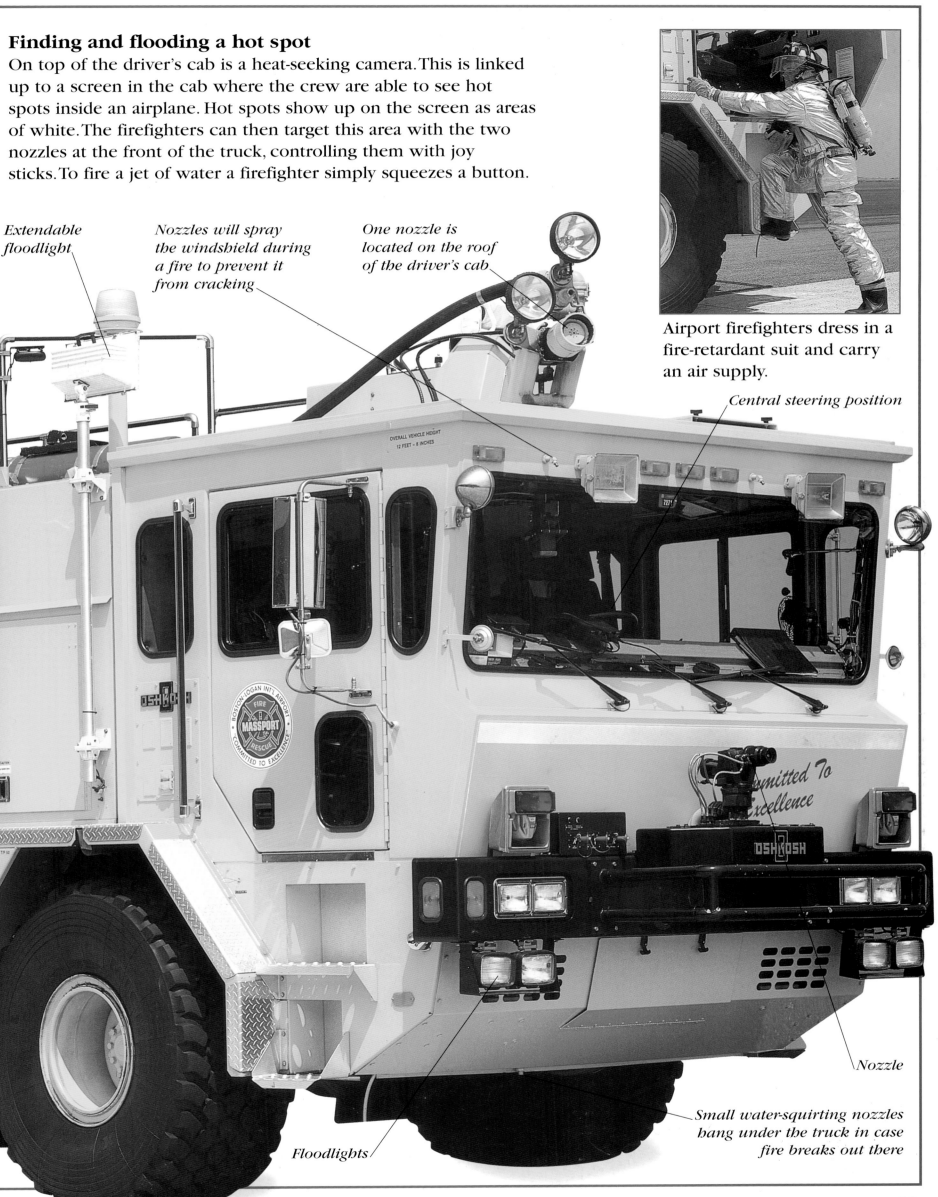

Airport firefighters dress in a fire-retardant suit and carry an air supply.

*Extendable floodlight*

*Nozzles will spray the windshield during a fire to prevent it from cracking*

*One nozzle is located on the roof of the driver's cab*

*Central steering position*

*Floodlights*

*Nozzle*

*Small water-squirting nozzles hang under the truck in case fire breaks out there*

# Stunt plane

Go to an air show and you'll see brightly colored planes zipping past, wing tips almost touching. Watch as highly trained pilots take the planes into intricate loops, rolls, and flips. It's an exciting sight when the stunt planes perform incredible air acrobatics.

One of the Red Arrows' most famous maneuvers is the Diamond Nine formation—a perfect diamond shape.

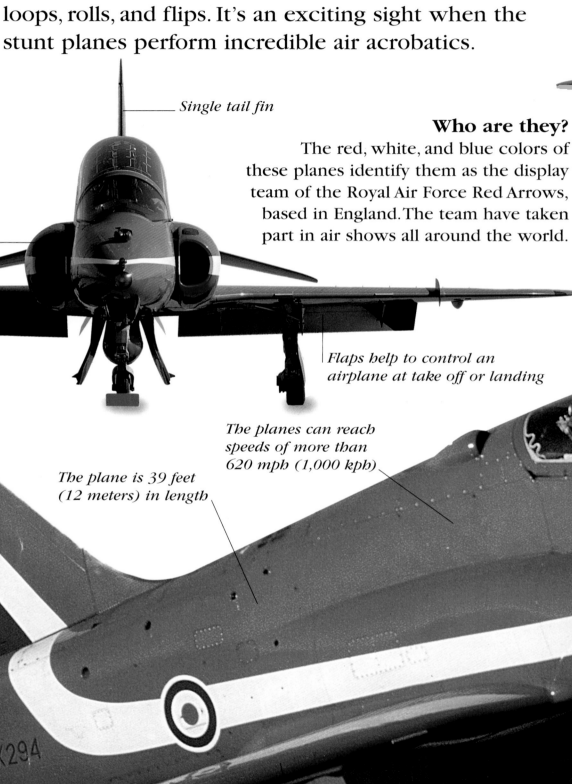

*Single tail fin*

*One of two semicircular air intakes*

**Who are they?**
The red, white, and blue colors of these planes identify them as the display team of the Royal Air Force Red Arrows, based in England. The team have taken part in air shows all around the world.

*The plane's wingspan is 31 feet (9.5 meters)*

*Flaps help to control an airplane at take off or landing*

*The planes can reach speeds of more than 620 mph (1,000 kph)*

*The plane is 39 feet (12 meters) in length*

*The rudder is used to control direction*

*Jet exhaust*

XX294

*The front of an airplane's wing is known as the leading edge. The back is the trailing edge*

*A wing fence improves the flow of air over the wing, helping lift*

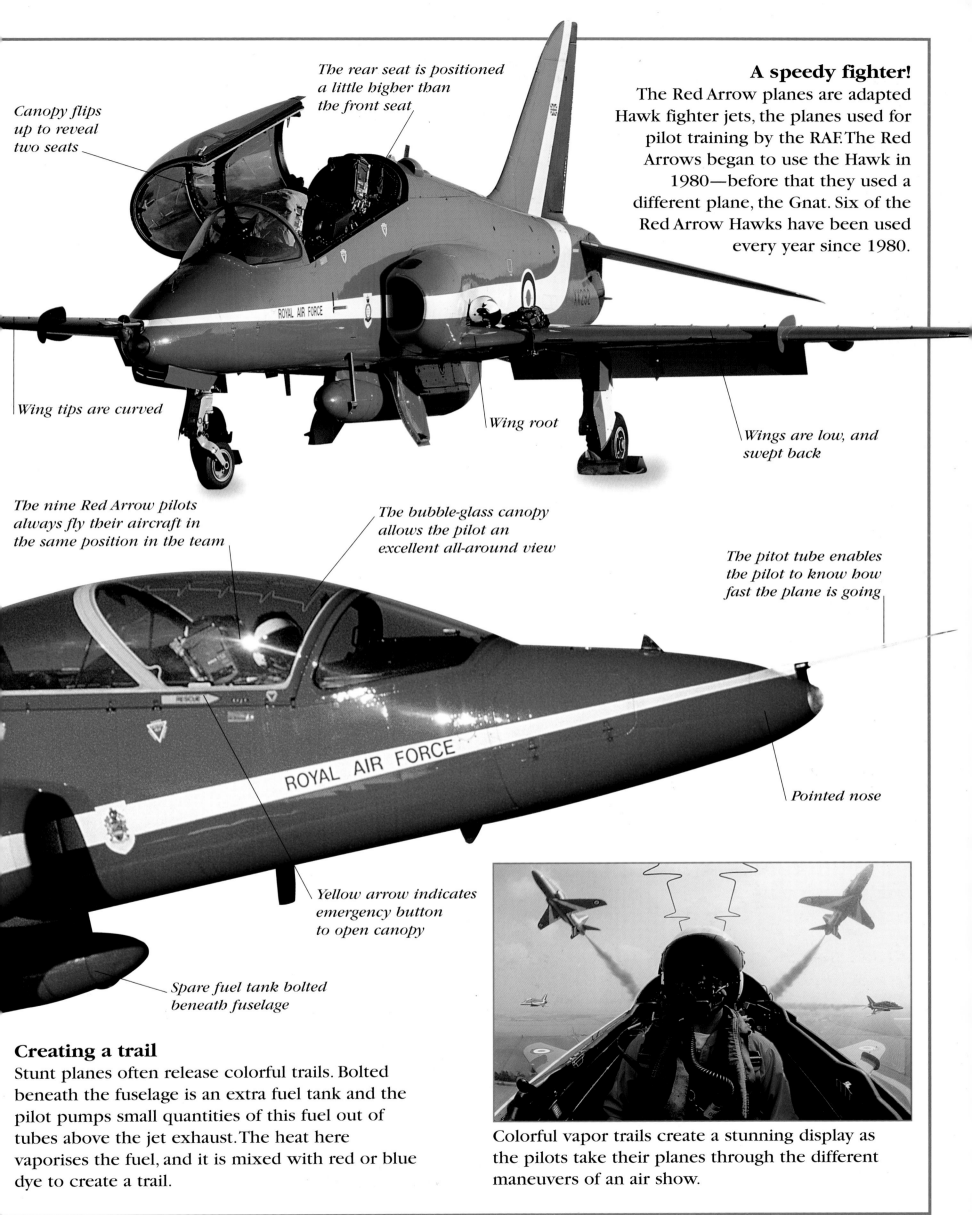

*Canopy flips up to reveal two seats*

*The rear seat is positioned a little higher than the front seat*

**A speedy fighter!**
The Red Arrow planes are adapted Hawk fighter jets, the planes used for pilot training by the RAF. The Red Arrows began to use the Hawk in 1980—before that they used a different plane, the Gnat. Six of the Red Arrow Hawks have been used every year since 1980.

*Wing tips are curved*

*Wing root*

*Wings are low, and swept back*

*The nine Red Arrow pilots always fly their aircraft in the same position in the team*

*The bubble-glass canopy allows the pilot an excellent all-around view*

*The pitot tube enables the pilot to know how fast the plane is going*

ROYAL AIR FORCE

*Pointed nose*

*Yellow arrow indicates emergency button to open canopy*

*Spare fuel tank bolted beneath fuselage*

### Creating a trail
Stunt planes often release colorful trails. Bolted beneath the fuselage is an extra fuel tank and the pilot pumps small quantities of this fuel out of tubes above the jet exhaust. The heat here vaporises the fuel, and it is mixed with red or blue dye to create a trail.

Colorful vapor trails create a stunning display as the pilots take their planes through the different maneuvers of an air show.

# Viper

Named after a dangerous type of snake, the Dodge Viper is one of the most spectacular cars ever built. It has an enormous engine which is more than six times bigger than the engine found in a small family car. In fact, it is one of the largest engines fitted to any car in the world, capable of taking the Viper to speeds exceeding 170 mph (274 kph). All big engines use a lot of fuel—driven fast the Viper only goes about six miles (two and half kilometers) on one gallon of gas!

**Pickup engine**
The engine for the Viper was converted from a pickup truck. The massive engine takes up a lot of room under the hood, so other equipment is squeezed into every available space.

**On the track**
The Viper is so fast that it is possible to use it for racing. It has successfully competed at races like the Le Mans 24 Hours in France, where it beat many "proper" racing cars.

*The Viper hood ornament is a snake.*

*All engines need far more air than gas, and the Viper is no exception. With its huge engine, the Viper can use more than 5,000 gallons (20,000 liters) of air every minute. These vents direct the air through the radiator to cool the engine.*

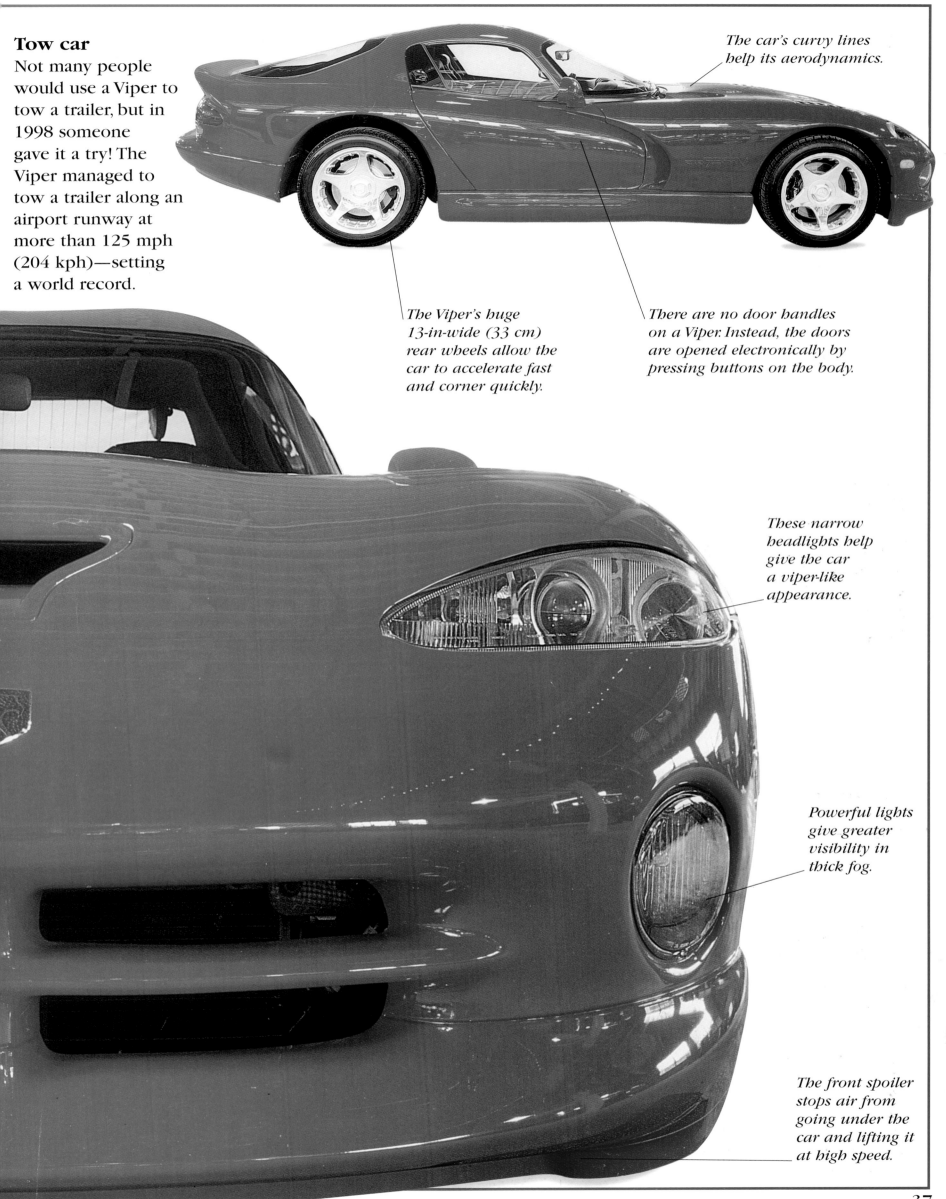

**Tow car**

Not many people would use a Viper to tow a trailer, but in 1998 someone gave it a try! The Viper managed to tow a trailer along an airport runway at more than 125 mph (204 kph)—setting a world record.

*The car's curvy lines help its aerodynamics.*

*The Viper's huge 13-in-wide (33 cm) rear wheels allow the car to accelerate fast and corner quickly.*

*There are no door handles on a Viper. Instead, the doors are opened electronically by pressing buttons on the body.*

*These narrow headlights help give the car a viper-like appearance.*

*Powerful lights give greater visibility in thick fog.*

*The front spoiler stops air from going under the car and lifting it at high speed.*

# Rescue hovercraft

If somebody needs help, but their boat is stuck on a shoal, a hovercraft is the only land-based vehicle that can easily reach them. This hovercraft can also negotiate high seas and strong winds to search for a boat in trouble. It is an incredible machine, happily passing over a variety of ground surfaces yet leaving less of an impression on sand than a footprint!

This small hovercraft is used as a rescue craft in Sweden, where it travels over ice.

*Radio antenna*

*Radar*

*This floodlight is so powerful that it is known as a "night sun"*

*A red light indicates that this is the port, or left-hand side, of the hovercraft*

*Flashing blue light*

*The craft's body is raised 4 feet (1.2 meters) when the skirt inflates*

*The pilot sits on the starboard, or right-hand side*

*Fender*

*Spray skirt*

EXTERNAL POWER

Canada

LIFERAFT

045

## Ready and waiting

Between rescue calls, the hovercraft is left open and ready to go. It is always refueled and its batteries recharged when it comes in. The crew of four can respond to a call and be on their way within seconds.

*A six-person life raft is stowed in this locker*

*A yellow light identifies the craft at night as a hovercraft*

*Three-bladed propeller*

*An anchor and line is kept in here in case of breakdown*

*Bow ramp*

*The hovercraft can travel onto land to pass a patient directly over to an ambulance crew*

*Emergency exit window*

## Floating on air

A hovercraft travels on a cushion of air, which is sucked in through a huge lift fan to fill the skirt. The skirt is made of strips of rubber fingers covered by a spray skirt. Altogether the craft is very fast and highly maneuverable.

*A gigantic lift fan 7 feet (2 meters) across is located under the exhaust pipe*

*Rudders are used for changes of direction*

*The engine is located here*

*Exhaust pipe*

*The hovercraft is able to tow a boat from its stern if necessary*

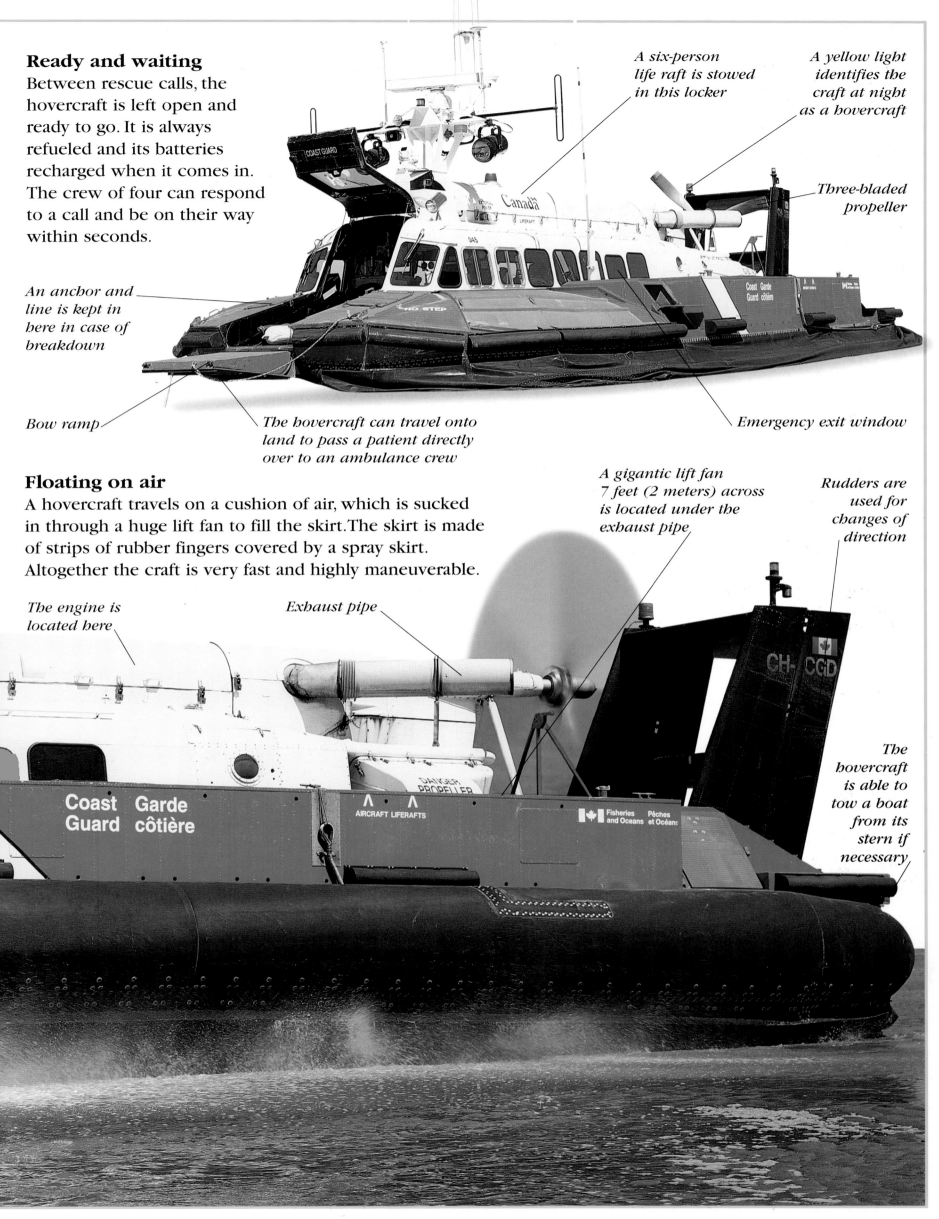

# Logging truck

Trucks delivering loads of lumber are a familiar sight in some areas. The planks are cut from tree trunks, and these are collected by powerful logging trucks. These trucks need to be powerful to transport 20 to 30 thick tree trunks along rough forest roads.

A truck like this hauls enough lumber planks to build a fence 600 ft (180 m) long.

*A metal plate protects the driver's cab from the logs*

*Side mirror*

*The manufacturer's symbol is displayed on the front of a truck*

Hayes

H321

### A long way down

A logging truck is heavy and potentially unstable, and its driver has to brake a lot on downhill runs out of forest areas. The trucks have extra-large tanks of water to cope with cooling the brakes on these journeys.

*Logs are loaded by the truck's own crane*

*Piles of logs ready to load onto the truck*

### A useful extra

Some logging trucks have built-in cranes to load and unload the logs. Others are loaded by separate cranes. On all logging trucks, the logs rest on bunks between tall metal stakes.

*Metal stake*

*Chains and metal ropes are used to secure the logs*

41

# Jumbo jet

The Boeing 747 is currently the largest of all airliners. That is why it is also known as the jumbo jet. After its introduction in 1969, it doubled the number of passengers that could be taken on one airplane. Most jumbos seat 420 passengers, but some have an internal layout that allows them to carry 569 passengers!

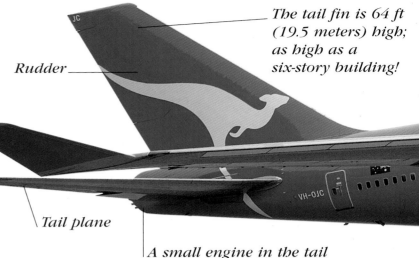

*The tail fin is 64 ft (19.5 meters) high; as high as a six-story building!*

*Rudder*

*Tail plane*

*A small engine in the tail powers the jumbo's electrical and air-conditioning systems when on the ground*

## Multi-purpose plane

The jumbo jet has been modified to perform a number of different tasks. Two jumbos have been adapted to ferry a NASA Space Shuttle to and from its launch site. They have been strengthened and have large struts to support the shuttle.

## Talking big

The jumbo jet has a massive 196-ft (60-meter) wingspan and a fuselage wide enough to seat ten passengers side by side—with space for two aisles. The passengers may be on board for 11 hours, so the plane will be loaded with more than 800 meals and about 30 gallons (120 liters) of juice and water. Everything about the plane is big!

*The fuselage wall is 7.5 in (19 cm) thick and includes a layer of sound and heat insulation*

*A wing's upper surface is curved more than its lower surface. As the engines push the plane forward, air rushing over the wings creates lift*

*In flight the winglet is angled downward, helping to direct air flow at the end of the wing*

*The four engines are attached to the lower side of the wings*

*An adult could stand up in the engine air intake*

*A jumbo jet's landing gear is tested to support double the weight of the jet*

*Each tire is four feet (1.25 meters) in diameter*

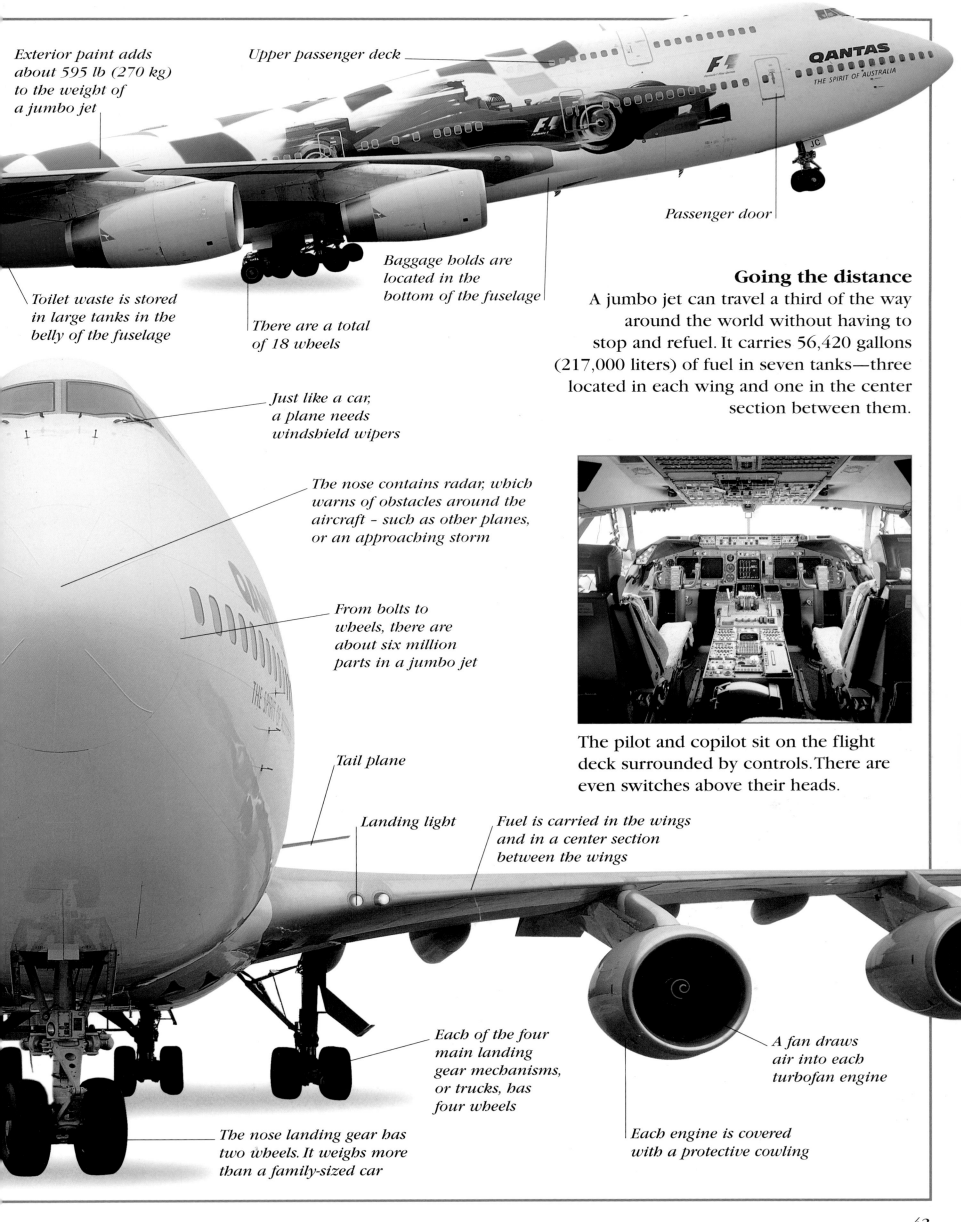

Exterior paint adds about 595 lb (270 kg) to the weight of a jumbo jet

Upper passenger deck

Toilet waste is stored in large tanks in the belly of the fuselage

There are a total of 18 wheels

Baggage holds are located in the bottom of the fuselage

Passenger door

### Going the distance

A jumbo jet can travel a third of the way around the world without having to stop and refuel. It carries 56,420 gallons (217,000 liters) of fuel in seven tanks—three located in each wing and one in the center section between them.

Just like a car, a plane needs windshield wipers

The nose contains radar, which warns of obstacles around the aircraft – such as other planes, or an approaching storm

From bolts to wheels, there are about six million parts in a jumbo jet

The pilot and copilot sit on the flight deck surrounded by controls. There are even switches above their heads.

Tail plane

Landing light

Fuel is carried in the wings and in a center section between the wings

Each of the four main landing gear mechanisms, or trucks, has four wheels

A fan draws air into each turbofan engine

The nose landing gear has two wheels. It weighs more than a family-sized car

Each engine is covered with a protective cowling

43

# Trucks

Trucks are everywhere, driving hundreds of miles every day and performing all kinds of tasks, from delivering goods to mixing concrete or lifting heavy equipment. They come in different sizes and shapes. But all trucks are basically the same, with a front section called a tractor and a rear one called a trailer, which varies with the truck's use.

## Where's the engine?

If a truck has a big hood to house the engine, the tractor unit is known as conventional or 'straight.' If the driver's cab is positioned directly above the engine, the tractor is known as forward control or 'cab-over.'

The tractor houses the engine

The semitrailer is supported at the back by its own axle and at the front by the tractor

An articulated truck can bend between the tractor and the trailer

The hood flips forward to reveal the engine

NILRAH EQUIPMENT, INC.
407-855-8700
ORLANDO, FL

This is a conventional tractor.

## To bend or not to bend

If a truck is articulated, the tractor and trailer can bend at the point where they join. The rear trailer is then known as a semitrailer, as it has no front wheels of its own and rests on a special 'fifth wheel' on the tractor. Other trucks are rigid. Rigid trucks are shorter than articulated trucks as they cannot bend around corners.

*This is a
cab-over tractor*

*The engine is
positioned beneath
the driver's cab*

1831

ACTROS

P424 LWF

# Wild Thing

Wild Thing was the first heavy-duty truck to take part in the Baja 1000, a famous race that takes place once a year on the California/Mexico border. The race covers 1000 kilometers, and it can take a grueling 18 hours. The driver and co-driver stay in their trucks most of this time, stopping just eight or nine times to refuel. It is a true endurance race over incredibly rough ground.

*Protective metal plate*

## Extra room

Wild Thing has much higher ground clearance than most trucks. It needs this to pass over uneven ground. A hefty metal plate protects the bottom from rocks.

*The windows do not have any glass, as it might shatter when the truck hits a bump*

*A bull bar helps to protect the front of the truck*

## Lightening the load

To prepare for the Baja race, Wild Thing's weight was lightened by stripping the truck of anything not required for racing. Engineers removed the equivalent in weight of 27 ten-year-old children!

**Valuable help**

Like most trucks today, Wild Thing has power steering, which makes the turns easier to handle. It is certainly needed to help maneuver around many obstacles.

*High wheel arches*

*The radiator fan has been repositioned at the back*

*The engine now sits behind the driver's cab*

*The battery stores electricity to start the engine*

*There is a large fuel tank on each side of the truck*

*The doors have been welded shut, so the driver and navigator climb in through the back of the truck*

*Shock absorbers allow the wheels to move up and down an incredible 21 in (53 cm)*

Trucks competing in the Baja 1000 often fly into the air as they come over the crest of a hill.

*A spare tire is important, despite its weight. It may be needed during the long race*

*The truck is equipped on a strong chassis*

*The wheels are the same as those used by ordinary trucks*

# Blackbird (SR-71A)

The Blackbird, or SR-71A, is a perfect spy plane. Not only can it fly at a jaw-dropping 2,000 mph (3,218 kph)—that's more than three times the speed of sound—its onboard cameras can read a license plate on a car from 17 miles (27 km) up! Now rarely used, the plane was first flown in the US in 1964.

*Red ribbons clearly indicate protective covers that have to be removed before take off*

On the way up, fuel streaks out. The plane's fuel tanks leak until they expand and seal as a result of high temperatures caused by speed.

*The whole rudder moves on a hinge at the base*

*Food is carried in tubes. The crew hold the tubes against the cockpit glass to warm the food!*

*The SR-71A carries a crew of two – a pilot and a reconnaissance systems officer*

*A curved edge, known as a chine, provides lift and stability to the front of the aircraft*

*Circular air intake (protected when on the ground) supplies air to the engine*

*Cone pulls back 26 in (66 cm) in flight, controlling the air allowed into the engine*

*Fuel more than doubles the empty weight of the plane*

*Landing lights*

*Front landing gear*

## Smash those records!
The Blackbird is one of the fastest jet-engine aircraft in the world. It set a number of world speed records in 1976, reaching 2,193 mph (3,530 kph). It also set an altitude record for a jet-engine aircraft of 85,069 feet (25,930 meters).

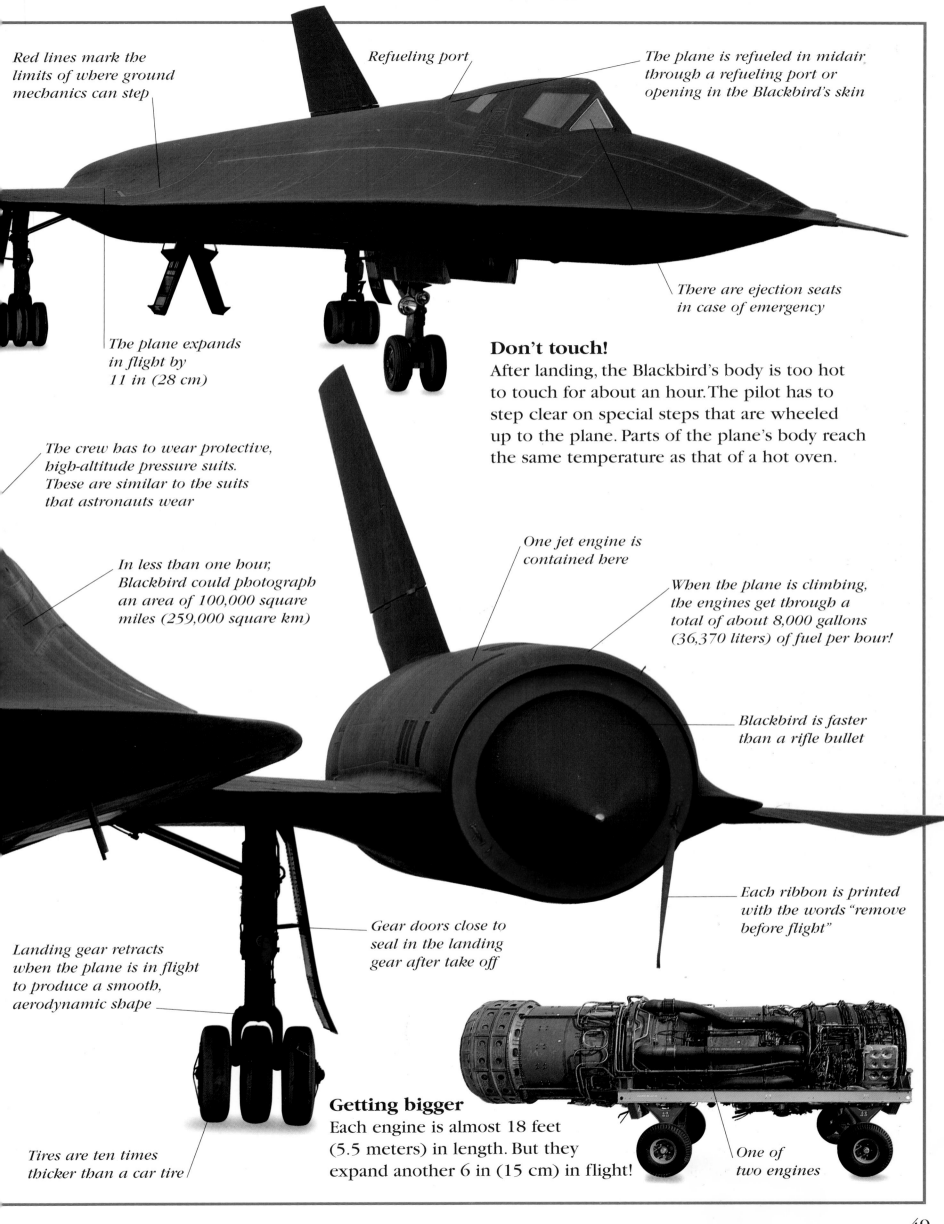

Red lines mark the limits of where ground mechanics can step

Refueling port

The plane is refueled in midair through a refueling port or opening in the Blackbird's skin

The plane expands in flight by 11 in (28 cm)

There are ejection seats in case of emergency

### Don't touch!
After landing, the Blackbird's body is too hot to touch for about an hour. The pilot has to step clear on special steps that are wheeled up to the plane. Parts of the plane's body reach the same temperature as that of a hot oven.

The crew has to wear protective, high-altitude pressure suits. These are similar to the suits that astronauts wear

In less than one hour, Blackbird could photograph an area of 100,000 square miles (259,000 square km)

One jet engine is contained here

When the plane is climbing, the engines get through a total of about 8,000 gallons (36,370 liters) of fuel per hour!

Blackbird is faster than a rifle bullet

Landing gear retracts when the plane is in flight to produce a smooth, aerodynamic shape

Gear doors close to seal in the landing gear after take off

Each ribbon is printed with the words "remove before flight"

Tires are ten times thicker than a car tire

### Getting bigger
Each engine is almost 18 feet (5.5 meters) in length. But they expand another 6 in (15 cm) in flight!

One of two engines

# Snow rescue vehicles

It can be difficult to mount a rescue operation in the snow. That's when a snowmobile can come in handy. The snowmobile's powerful motor drives a caterpillar track under the machine and propels it over the snow and ice. The driver grips handlebars attached to two metal skis at the front of the machine to carefully guide the snowmobile over the frozen landscape.

*The hatch opens upward for easy access*

*There is no room for a first-aid kit – the casualty is taken straight to the hospital*

*A stretcher slides in and out through the hatch*

## Hidden away

The snowmobile hauls a rescue sled. Open the back of the sled and there's room inside for a casualty to ride on a stretcher. The stretcher has straps to keep the casualty immobile.

*A small windshield helps to protect the paramedic when he is driving*

*The throttle is controlled with the right hand*

*There are no indicators, just a pair of headlights*

*The paramedic turns the handlebars to turn the front skis*

*The handbrake is controlled with the left hand*

*Polaris*

*E 5725*

## Fire rescue all-terrain vehicle

This unusual vehicle is used for the rescue of people and trapped animals in a mountainous area of Australia. It carries four firefighters, and plenty of rescue equipment and firefighting hoses. The rubber caterpillar tracks do less damage to the ground than tires or metal tracks. That makes it good for use in areas where ground erosion is a problem.

Floodlight

The crew travels in the front section

Access ladder to roof of trailer

Equipment trailer

Spotlights are essential for lighting a scene at night

The tractor unit and trailer are both on caterpillar tracks

The paramedic wears protective clothing

The rescue sled is long enough to hold a person on a stretcher

A waterproof cover protects the occupant from snow

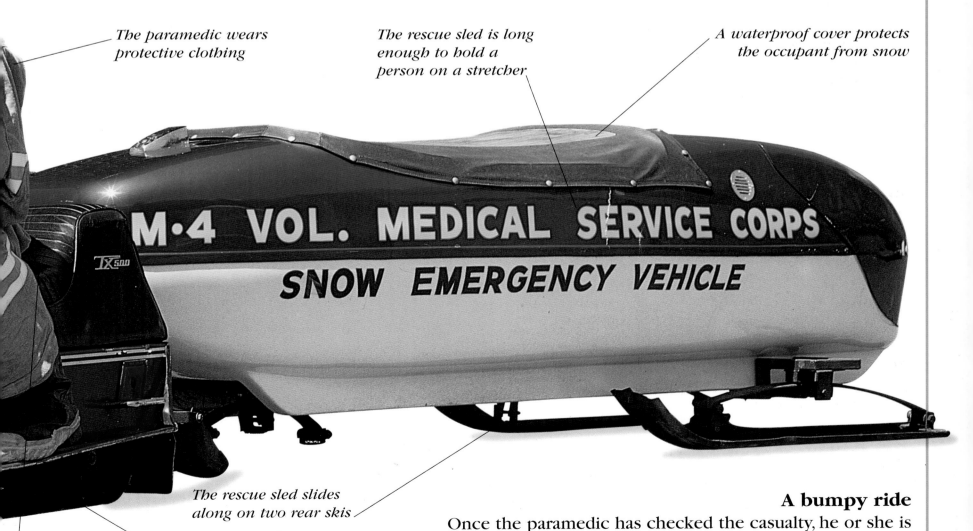

M·4 VOL. MEDICAL SERVICE CORPS

SNOW EMERGENCY VEHICLE

The rescue sled slides along on two rear skis

Caterpillar tracks

The paramedic sits above the fuel tank

### A bumpy ride

Once the paramedic has checked the casualty, he or she is strapped to the stretcher, the back is secured, and the paramedic sets off for the hospital. It can be a bumpy ride, as snow can hide debris on the path, so the paramedic will drive fairly slowly.

# Fireboat

Fires occasionally break out in buildings right next to harbors, or on boats. A fireboat can flood these fires within seconds as water is pumped directly from the endless supply surrounding the boat.

The fireboat can pump about 7,500 gallons (34,000 liters) of water a minute. That's five times more than a large fire engine you'll see on the street.

*The wheelhouse nozzle can telescope up about 12 feet (3 meters)*

*Radar*

*The main steering position is inside the wheelhouse*

*Searchlight*

*Blue flashing light*

*Exhaust pipes*

*There are steering positions on either side of the wheelhouse*

*A roof-mounted observation window allows the crew to view the aerial nozzle*

## Rapid response

The fireboat has three massive engines, the combined power of which is at least ten times more powerful than the engine on a large fire truck. The engines propel the boat through the water. The pilot has to keep a sharp lookout for other watercraft.

*The boat can also be controlled from the aft, or rear, steering station*

*Hoses can be attached here*

*The fireboat creates a large wake as it surges through the water*

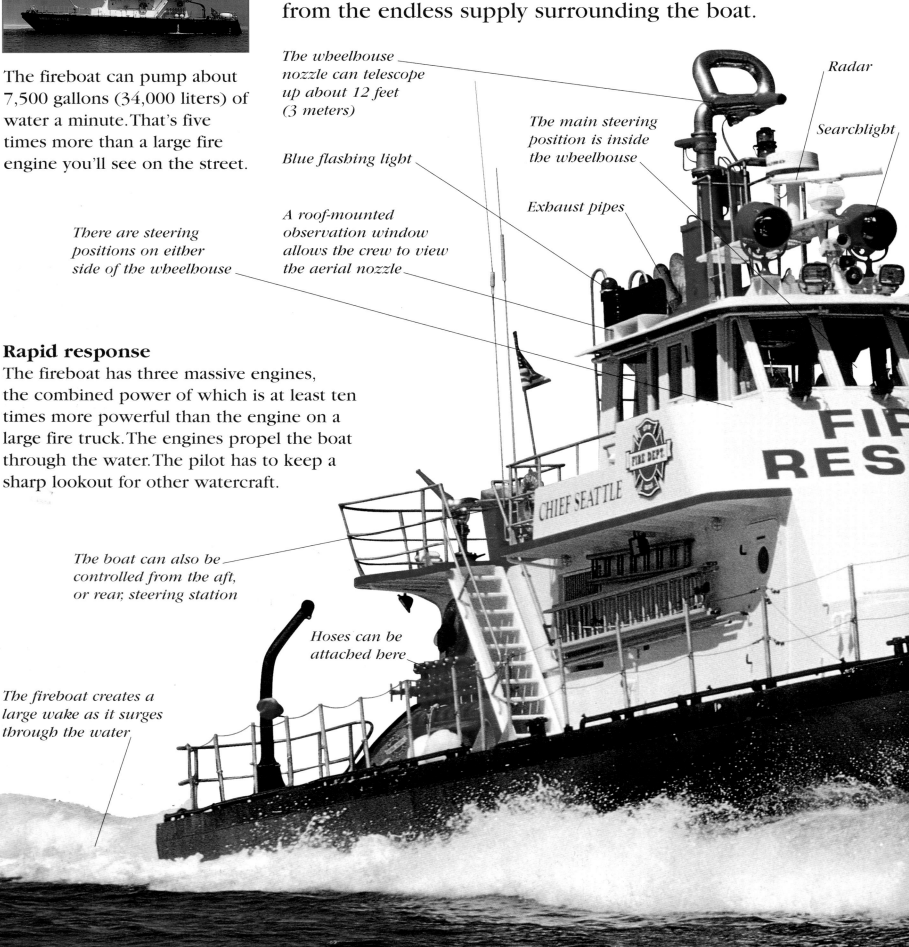

CHIEF SEATTLE

FIRE DEP'T

FIR RES

The fireboat carries many of the things an ordinary fire engine would carry, including fire suits and boots, protective helmets, shovels, hoses, a chain saw, and ladders.

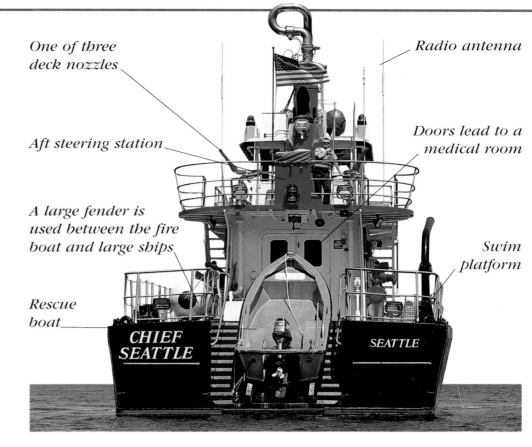

One of three deck nozzles

Radio antenna

Aft steering station

Doors lead to a medical room

A large fender is used between the fire boat and large ships

Swim platform

Rescue boat

CHIEF SEATTLE

SEATTLE

## Extra help

A small rescue/under pier boat is carried at the stern of the boat. It may be used to take a hose under a pier or bridge or to rescue people from the water. It is winched down a ramp and passes over a swim platform to reach the water.

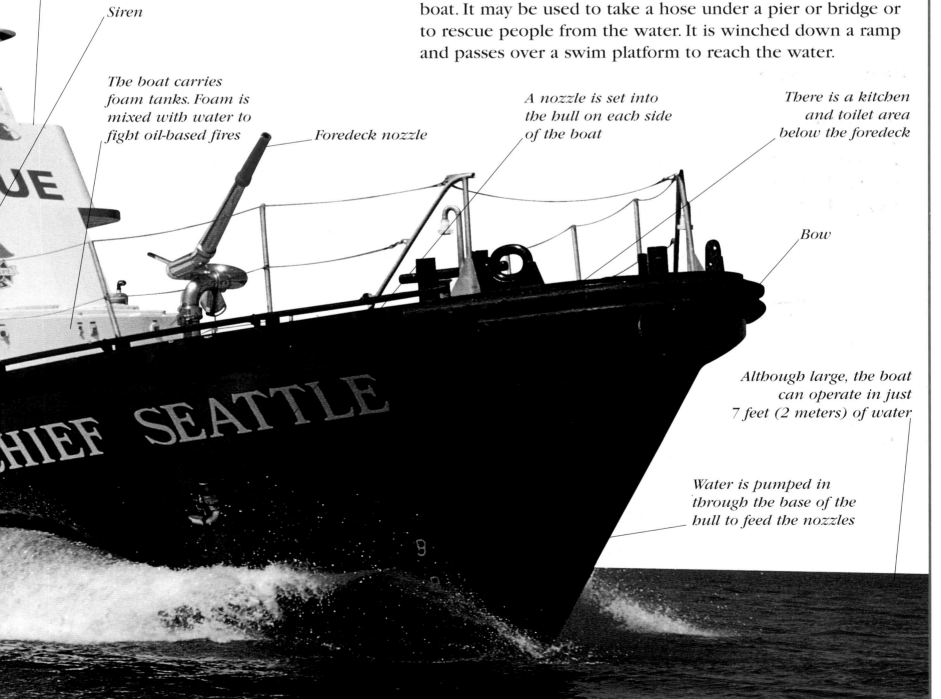

Port steering position

Siren

The boat carries foam tanks. Foam is mixed with water to fight oil-based fires

Foredeck nozzle

A nozzle is set into the hull on each side of the boat

There is a kitchen and toilet area below the foredeck

Bow

Although large, the boat can operate in just 7 feet (2 meters) of water

Water is pumped in through the base of the hull to feed the nozzles

CHIEF SEATTLE

# Formula One

Formula One cars are the most advanced technically of all race cars, and can reach speeds of up to 210 mph (340 kph) on a racetrack. The best drivers from all around the world compete in as many as 17 races in one season. The races take place in 16 countries across five continents. So the winner really deserves to be called the World Motor Racing Champion!

## Hand-built
The Jaguar Formula One car starts its life as a drawing on a computer screen. It takes skilled mechanics up to nine months to attach the 3,500 individual parts that make up the race car!

## No expense spared!
All the teams racing in Formula One build their own cars in specially designed workshops. Each car is made from very expensive materials that are both light and strong, such as titanium and carbon fiber. To design a car, buy the materials, and then build it costs several million dollars, and a team can need up to nine cars in one season!

*Over 2,500 new tires are taken to every Formula One race*

*The car's body is made of carbon fiber*

*Different front wings are used for long, fast tracks and short, twisty ones*

*The aerodynamic shape of the nose cone allows air to flow over the front wing*

*This is where the jack lifts the front of the car during the pit stops*

_Front wing_

_Rear wing_

## On the track

Airplanes use wings to lift them into the air. Formula One cars also use wings, but they are turned over so that instead of lifting, the wings help to keep the car on the track.

_There is an onboard camera on each car_

_The driver uses these paddles behind the steering wheel to change gear_

_During a race, the tire gets very hot, and this helps the car to grip the track_

_The bodywork is less than 2 inches (4 centimeters) above the track surface_

_This rod operates one of the very stiff suspension springs—Formula One cars are built for speed not comfort!_

A race can be won or lost on a pit stop. So trained mechanics work at lightning speed to change the tires and refuel in a matter of seconds!

# Bullet trains

The futuristic-looking, high-speed electric trains that run in Japan are called Bullet trains. Their Japanese name is Shinkansen. First introduced in 1964, the trains provided the first passenger service in the world to travel at speeds of 100 miles (161 kilometers) per hour. Today, the trains reach much faster speeds of up to 190 miles (300 kilometers) per hour, running on specially designed tracks. Bullet trains also offer very frequent service, and carry nearly one million passengers a day.

**Speeding past Mount Fuji**
This modern type of Bullet train is made of aluminum alloy for lightness and speed.

**High-speed journey**
The Series 100 Bullet train has a top speed of 141 miles (228 kilometers) per hour. It has cut the intercity time from Tokyo to Osaka, a distance of 321 miles (516 kilometers), to three hours.

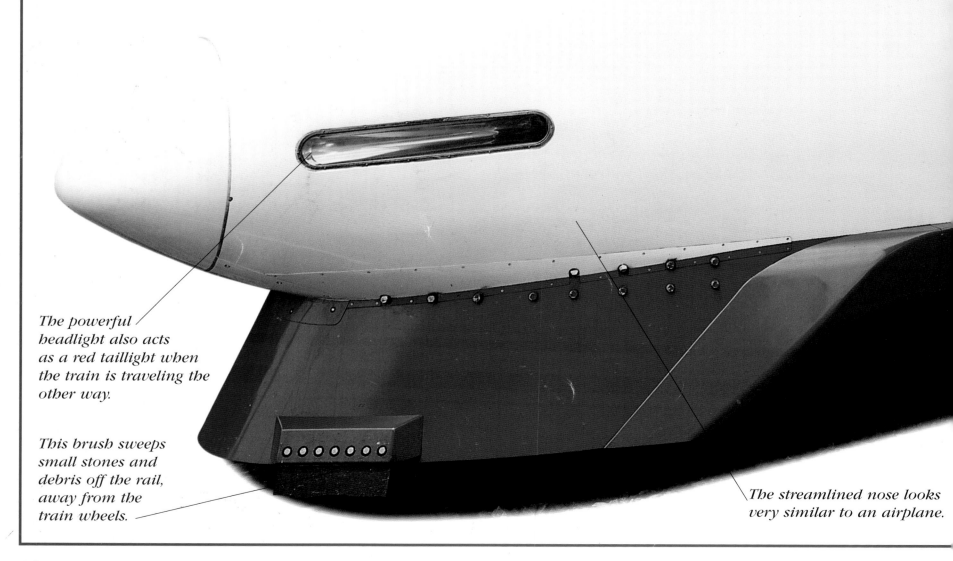

*The driver sits high up and has a clear view of the line ahead.*

*The powerful headlight also acts as a red taillight when the train is traveling the other way.*

*This brush sweeps small stones and debris off the rail, away from the train wheels.*

*The streamlined nose looks very similar to an airplane.*

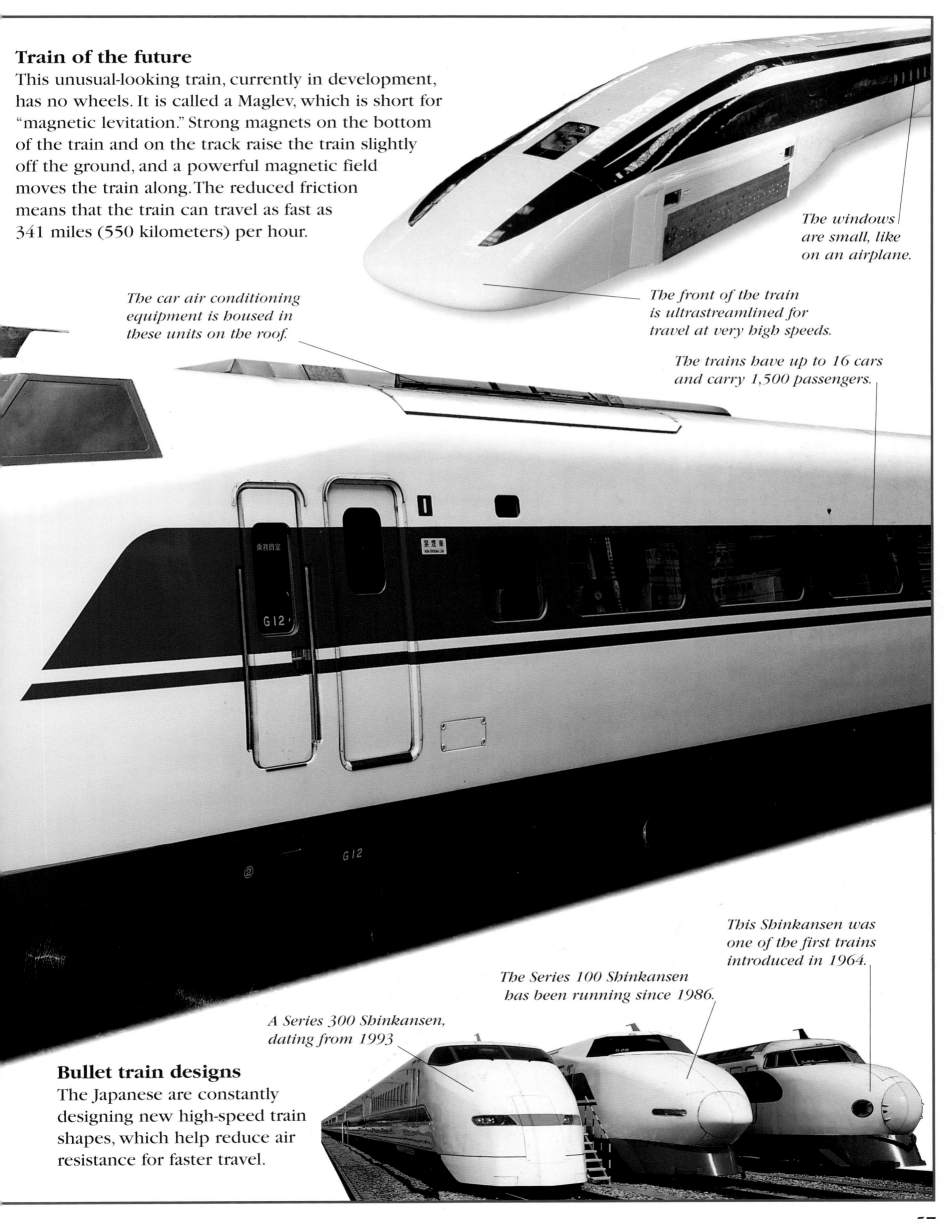

## Train of the future

This unusual-looking train, currently in development, has no wheels. It is called a Maglev, which is short for "magnetic levitation." Strong magnets on the bottom of the train and on the track raise the train slightly off the ground, and a powerful magnetic field moves the train along. The reduced friction means that the train can travel as fast as 341 miles (550 kilometers) per hour.

*The windows are small, like on an airplane.*

*The front of the train is ultrastreamlined for travel at very high speeds.*

*The car air conditioning equipment is housed in these units on the roof.*

*The trains have up to 16 cars and carry 1,500 passengers.*

*This Shinkansen was one of the first trains introduced in 1964.*

*The Series 100 Shinkansen has been running since 1986.*

*A Series 300 Shinkansen, dating from 1993*

## Bullet train designs

The Japanese are constantly designing new high-speed train shapes, which help reduce air resistance for faster travel.

# Fire truck

Everybody recognizes the wail of a fire truck's siren. It warns drivers to move out of the way because the fire truck is in a hurry. There may be a fire, or somebody may be stuck in a tree. This fire truck has a platform on the end of a ladder. It is used to lift firefighters high into the air.

*Serving Since 1889* **ABERDEEN** 102 FT

### Going up—or down!

An aerial platform telescopes out and up on the end of a long boom. This one can be raised 102 feet (31 meters): as high as a 7-story building. The ladder can also rotate 360 degrees. It can even drop down to allow people to step off at ground level.

TRUCK 231

ABERDEEN FIRE DEPT.

*Outriggers provide stability*

*Fixed floodlight*

*This bag can be carried into an apartment. It contains small hoses*

*This panel controls the air supply from the oxygen bottle to the platform*

*Oxygen bottle*

*The boom rests on a plate that can turn a complete circle*

102 FT

ABERDE

TRUCK

EMERGENCY 911

HARFORD COU

*Fold down step for access to boom*

*Exhaust pipe*

*Water intake valve*

*Water discharge valve*

*Two crew members can sit in here*

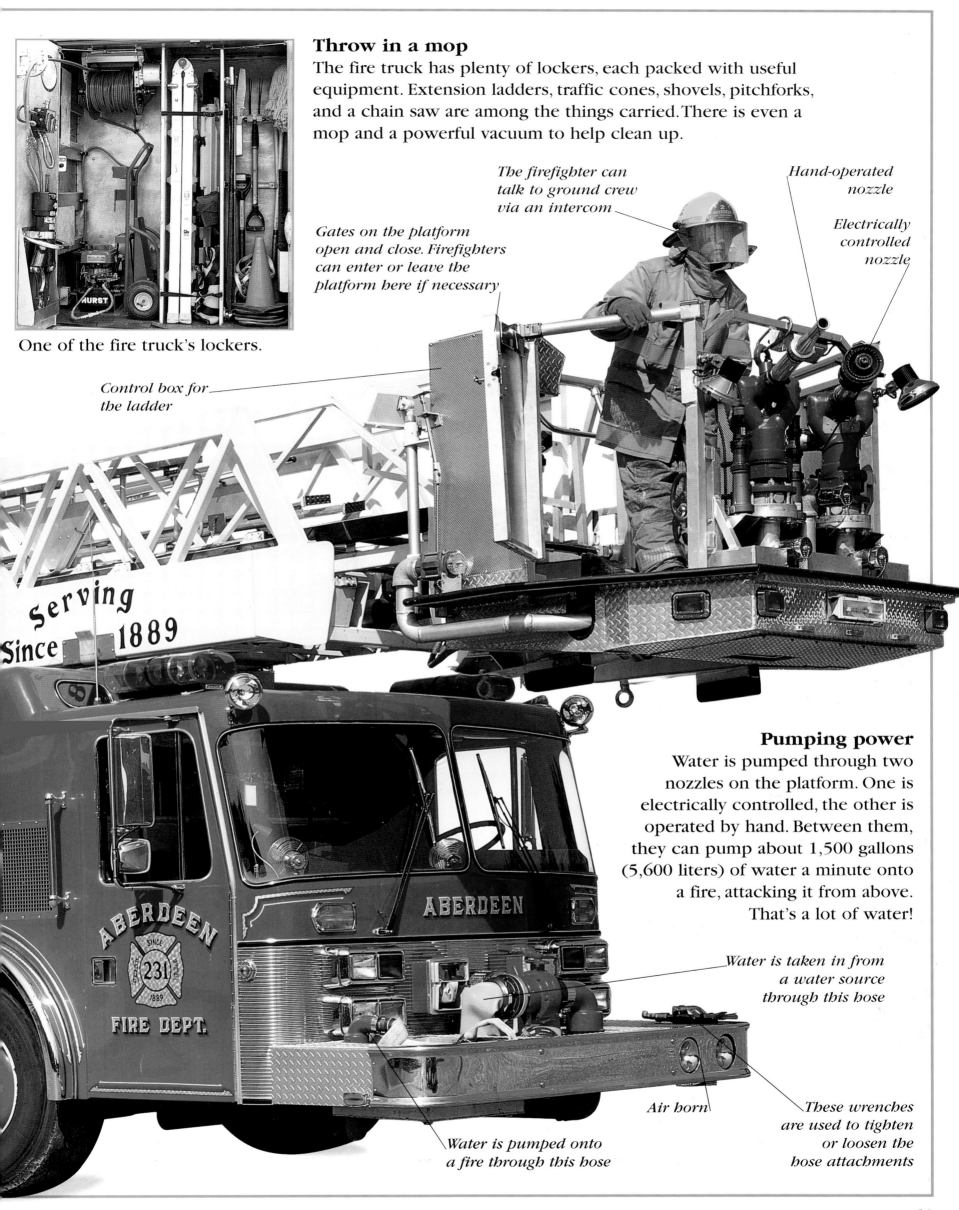

## Throw in a mop

The fire truck has plenty of lockers, each packed with useful equipment. Extension ladders, traffic cones, shovels, pitchforks, and a chain saw are among the things carried. There is even a mop and a powerful vacuum to help clean up.

One of the fire truck's lockers.

*The firefighter can talk to ground crew via an intercom*

*Gates on the platform open and close. Firefighters can enter or leave the platform here if necessary*

*Control box for the ladder*

*Hand-operated nozzle*

*Electrically controlled nozzle*

Serving Since 1889

ABERDEEN

ABERDEEN
SINCE
231
1889
FIRE DEPT.

## Pumping power

Water is pumped through two nozzles on the platform. One is electrically controlled, the other is operated by hand. Between them, they can pump about 1,500 gallons (5,600 liters) of water a minute onto a fire, attacking it from above. That's a lot of water!

*Water is taken in from a water source through this hose*

*Air horn*

*These wrenches are used to tighten or loosen the hose attachments*

*Water is pumped onto a fire through this hose*

# Gee Bee

Take a massive engine, add a pair of unusually short wings, and allow a tiny space for the pilot's cockpit. The result will probably look something like the spectacular Gee Bee Super Sportster, a plane that thrilled air-racing crowds in 1930s America with its extraordinary speed and daredevil tactics.

This Gee Bee has reached a top speed of 190 mph (305 kph).

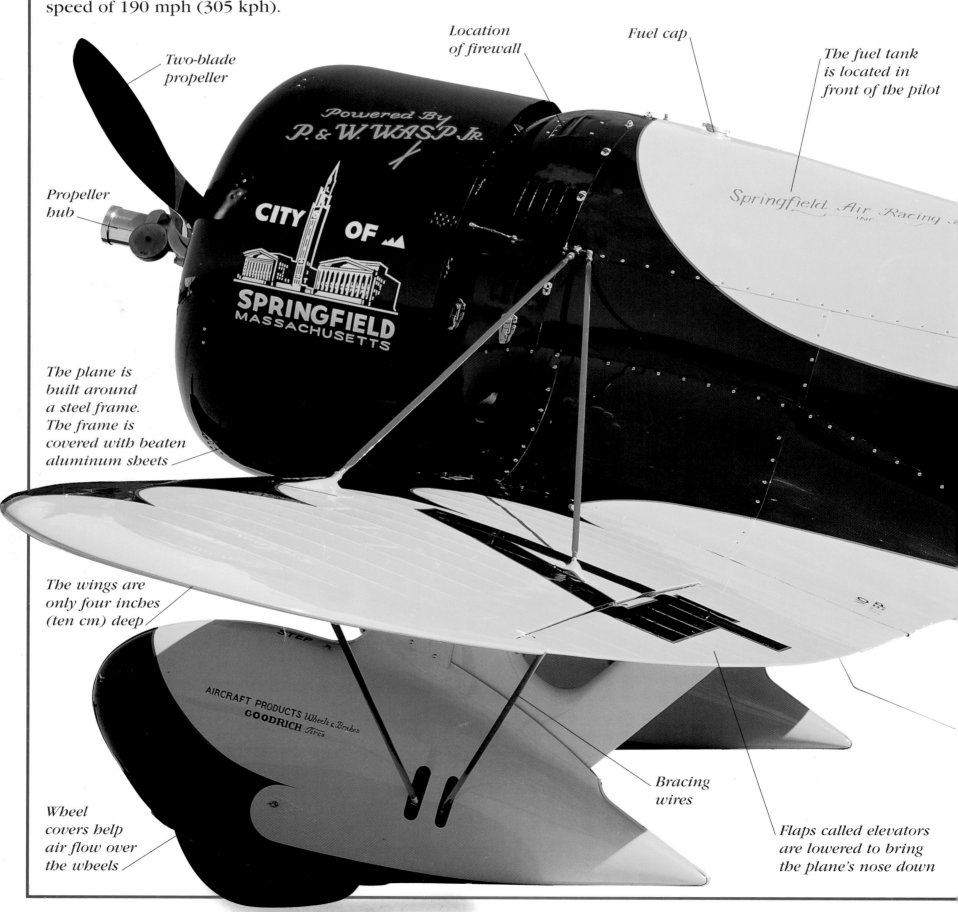

Two-blade propeller

Propeller hub

The plane is built around a steel frame. The frame is covered with beaten aluminum sheets

The wings are only four inches (ten cm) deep

Wheel covers help air flow over the wheels

Location of firewall

Fuel cap

The fuel tank is located in front of the pilot

Powered By P. & W. WASP Jr.

CITY OF SPRINGFIELD MASSACHUSETTS

Springfield Air Racing INC

AIRCRAFT PRODUCTS Wheels & Brakes GOODRICH Tires

Bracing wires

Flaps called elevators are lowered to bring the plane's nose down

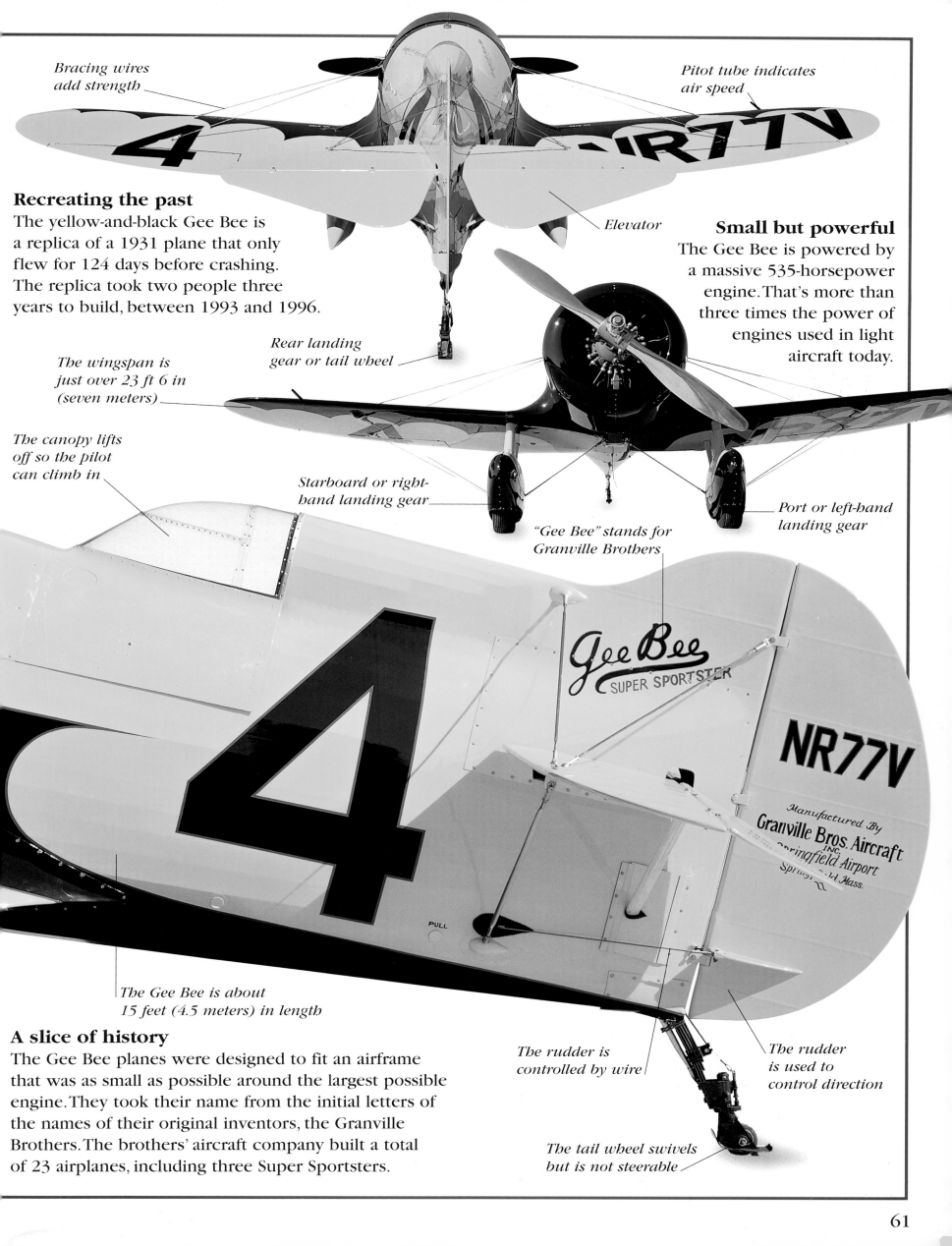

Bracing wires
add strength

Pitot tube indicates
air speed

## Recreating the past
The yellow-and-black Gee Bee is
a replica of a 1931 plane that only
flew for 124 days before crashing.
The replica took two people three
years to build, between 1993 and 1996.

Elevator

## Small but powerful
The Gee Bee is powered by
a massive 535-horsepower
engine. That's more than
three times the power of
engines used in light
aircraft today.

Rear landing
gear or tail wheel

The wingspan is
just over 23 ft 6 in
(seven meters)

The canopy lifts
off so the pilot
can climb in

Starboard or right-
hand landing gear

Port or left-hand
landing gear

"Gee Bee" stands for
Granville Brothers

Gee Bee
SUPER SPORTSTER

NR77V

Manufactured By
Granville Bros. Aircraft
INC.
Springfield Airport
Springfield, Mass.

PULL

The Gee Bee is about
15 feet (4.5 meters) in length

## A slice of history
The Gee Bee planes were designed to fit an airframe
that was as small as possible around the largest possible
engine. They took their name from the initial letters of
the names of their original inventors, the Granville
Brothers. The brothers' aircraft company built a total
of 23 airplanes, including three Super Sportsters.

The rudder is
controlled by wire

The rudder
is used to
control direction

The tail wheel swivels
but is not steerable

# Superbike

Superbike races attract enormous crowds all around the world. One of the reasons for this popularity is that the bikes are based on the machines we see on the road every day. This does not mean they are slow—Superbikes can lap some racetracks as fast as 500cc Grand Prix bikes!

Superbike riders have special pads on their leather suits to allow their knees to slide along the track.

### Much more than a road bike
Superbikes look like road bikes, but in fact nearly every part is different. Specially manufactured, very expensive racing components make the Superbike much faster than the road version.

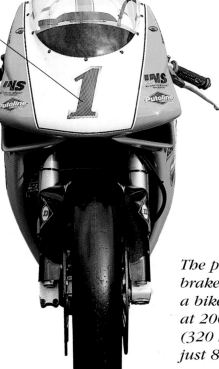

*The number 1 shows that this is the champion's bike*

### Through the air
A narrow bike will move through the air more easily than a wider one, so designers try to make their bikes as narrow as possible. The top Superbikes use very slim engines, and this helps the designers to minimize the width of the bike.

*The powerful brakes can stop a bike traveling at 200 mph (320 kph) in just 8 seconds*

The tank must be big enough to carry fuel for the whole race because there are no pit stops

The seat padding is very thin, but the rider only sits on it along the straights

Special racing mufflers make the Superbike much louder than a road bike

*Sprocket*

### How fast?
Even the fastest racing bikes will never achieve the lap times set by the best racing cars because cars go around corners much faster than bikes. But in a straight line, this bike is nearly as fast as a Formula One car and can reach speeds of up to 200 mph (320 kph)!

The rider operates the gear lever with his foot

The footrest is in this high position so that it does not touch the racetrack on corners

These smooth tires can only be used on dry tracks

# Pink Cadillac

At a time when American cars were big and luxurious, the Cadillac was the biggest and most luxurious of all. This convertible version cost three times as much as a family car. It was made when air travel by jet was just starting and was designed to attract attention by looking like a jet plane. It attracted even more attention when it was pink!

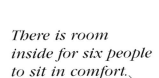

*There is room inside for six people to sit in comfort.*

**Cadillac interior**
Everything was done to make driving the Cadillac as effortless as possible. Adjusting the seat, lowering the roof, and opening the trunk were all done electrically. Even the headlights dimmed automatically!

*A Cadillac was the first car to be fitted with twin headlights.*

*The surrounds of the lights resemble the air intake of a jet engine.*

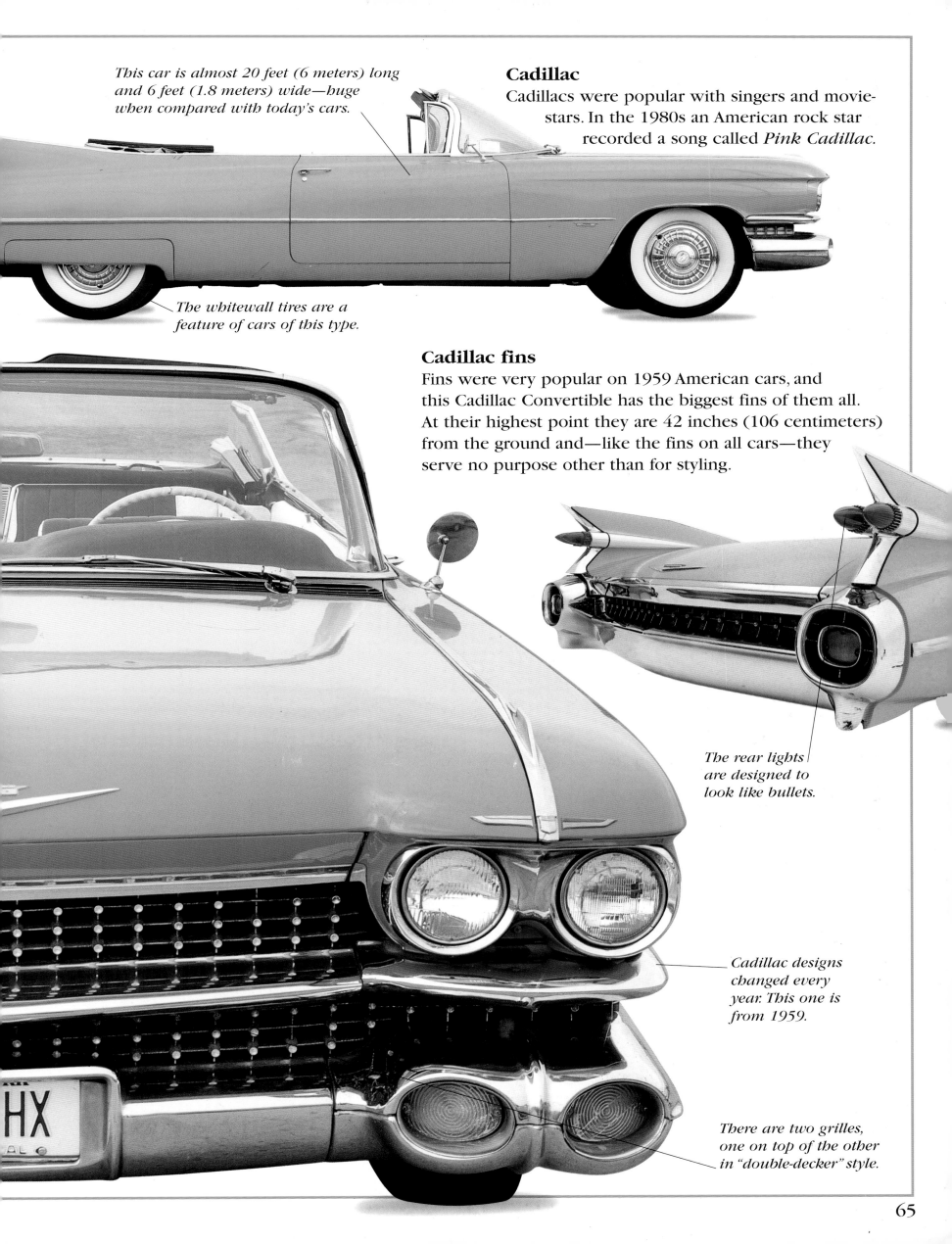

This car is almost 20 feet (6 meters) long and 6 feet (1.8 meters) wide—huge when compared with today's cars.

## Cadillac

Cadillacs were popular with singers and movie-stars. In the 1980s an American rock star recorded a song called *Pink Cadillac*.

The whitewall tires are a feature of cars of this type.

## Cadillac fins

Fins were very popular on 1959 American cars, and this Cadillac Convertible has the biggest fins of them all. At their highest point they are 42 inches (106 centimeters) from the ground and—like the fins on all cars—they serve no purpose other than for styling.

The rear lights are designed to look like bullets.

Cadillac designs changed every year. This one is from 1959.

There are two grilles, one on top of the other in "double-decker" style.

# Concrete mixer truck

The big drum of this concrete mixer truck rolls around and around as the truck travels to a building site. The rolling motion churns up the wet concrete that's inside, mixing it well and keeping it from setting. It's a little like a gigantic cake mixer—but if this mixer stopped turning, the concrete would quickly set rock hard.

## A perfect mix

Six tons of sand are required for every concrete mix—that's the same weight as 6 family cars! Throw in 6 tons of gravel, 1½ tons of cement, and 132 gallons (500 liters) of water. Mix well and you have wet concrete.

Cab-over tractor

Water is pumped into the drum from the water tank when the truck nears its destination

Water tank

The drum rests on a strong steel frame called a chassis

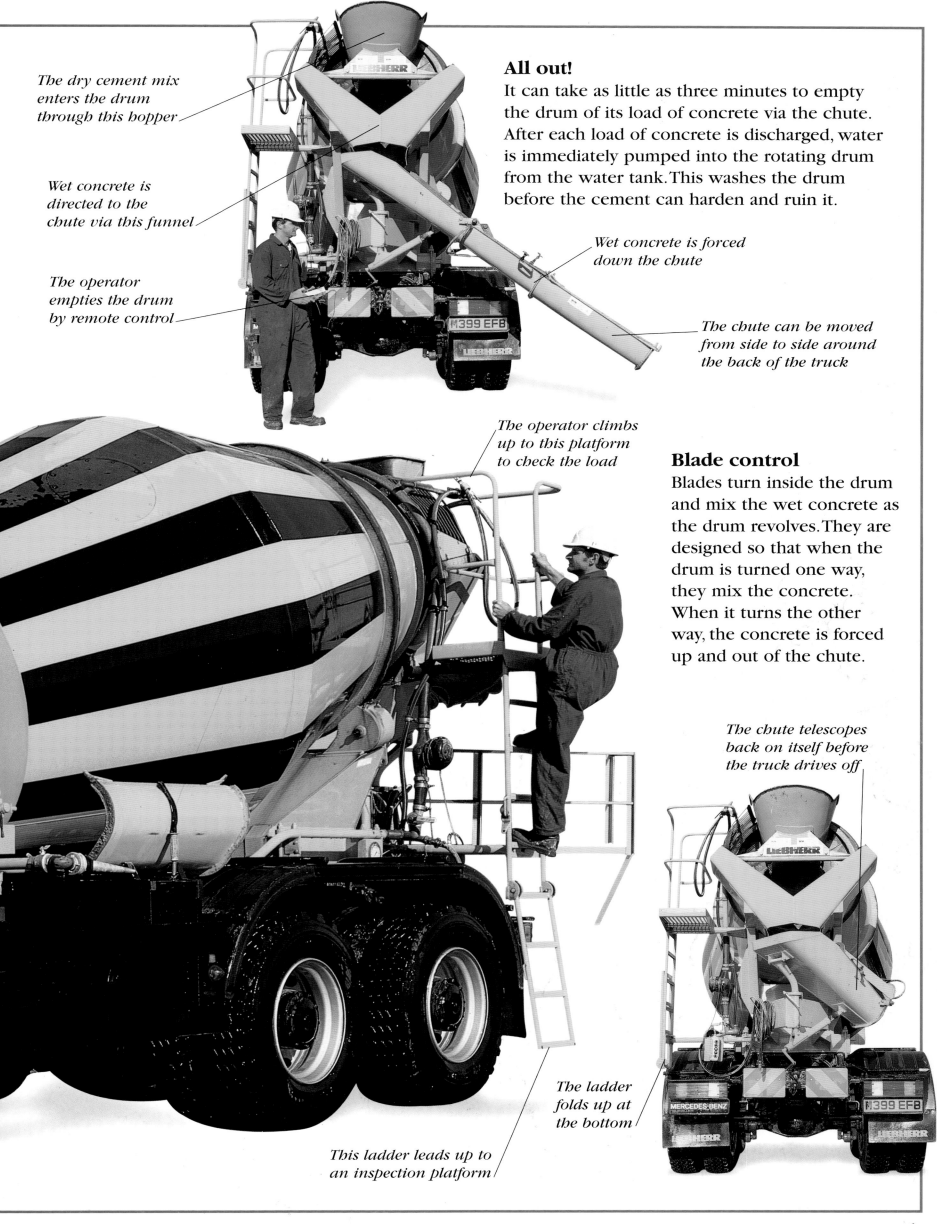

The dry cement mix enters the drum through this hopper

Wet concrete is directed to the chute via this funnel

The operator empties the drum by remote control

## All out!

It can take as little as three minutes to empty the drum of its load of concrete via the chute. After each load of concrete is discharged, water is immediately pumped into the rotating drum from the water tank. This washes the drum before the cement can harden and ruin it.

Wet concrete is forced down the chute

The chute can be moved from side to side around the back of the truck

The operator climbs up to this platform to check the load

## Blade control

Blades turn inside the drum and mix the wet concrete as the drum revolves. They are designed so that when the drum is turned one way, they mix the concrete. When it turns the other way, the concrete is forced up and out of the chute.

The chute telescopes back on itself before the truck drives off

This ladder leads up to an inspection platform

The ladder folds up at the bottom

*Raised canopy*

*Instructor pilot*

*Trainee pilot*

# F-16

The F-16 is a multi-role fighter aircraft, originally designed for close-up air combat. It is also used for air-to-ground attack. It has excellent maneuverability. Flying at a height of 7.5 miles (12 km), an F-16 can reach a speed of 1,350 mph (2,172 kph), or just over twice the speed of sound. The F-16 is officially known as the Fighting Falcon, but all the pilots call it the Viper.

RESCUE

FORCE

*This specially adapted pitot tube is only used for flight tests*

**Getting ready to go**
The pilots and ground crew have lots of checks to complete before they are ready to take off. These take them about 45 minutes—they check everything, including the flight controls.

*Forward landing gear*

*The cockpit is equipped with a visual display screen known as a Heads-Up-Display. It tells the pilots where they are and displays weapons and targeting information*

*Pitot tube*

78-0098   MAJ. ROB ADAM

RESCUE

1. PUSH BUTTON TO OPEN DOOR
2. PULL RING OUT 6 FEET TO JETTISON CANOPY

*A bright yellow arrow points to a handle. Ground personnel pull this to jettison the canopy in an emergency*

*The first F-16s had black radomes (or radar covers). Pilots felt it was an easy target for enemy fire, so the black was changed to gray*

*The forward landing gear retracts into a compartment in flight*

The F-16 is the most commonly flown aircraft in the US Air Force. It is also used in many other countries.

*The F-16 has a unique flight control system known as fly-by-wire. It means that computers and electronics have replaced many of the older-style mechanical workings*

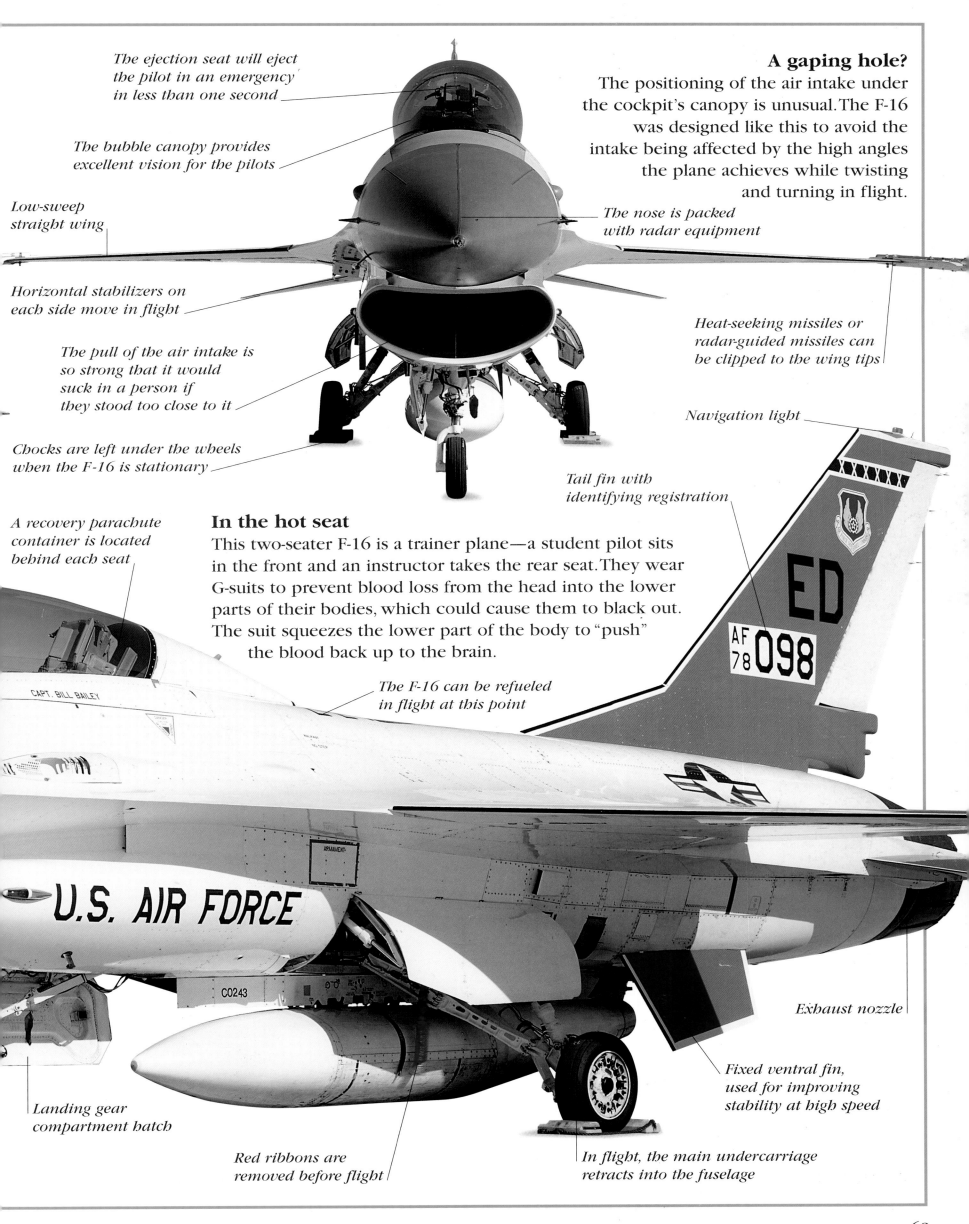

The ejection seat will eject the pilot in an emergency in less than one second

The bubble canopy provides excellent vision for the pilots

Low-sweep straight wing

Horizontal stabilizers on each side move in flight

The pull of the air intake is so strong that it would suck in a person if they stood too close to it

Chocks are left under the wheels when the F-16 is stationary

A recovery parachute container is located behind each seat

## A gaping hole?

The positioning of the air intake under the cockpit's canopy is unusual. The F-16 was designed like this to avoid the intake being affected by the high angles the plane achieves while twisting and turning in flight.

The nose is packed with radar equipment

Heat-seeking missiles or radar-guided missiles can be clipped to the wing tips

Navigation light

Tail fin with identifying registration

## In the hot seat

This two-seater F-16 is a trainer plane—a student pilot sits in the front and an instructor takes the rear seat. They wear G-suits to prevent blood loss from the head into the lower parts of their bodies, which could cause them to black out. The suit squeezes the lower part of the body to "push" the blood back up to the brain.

The F-16 can be refueled in flight at this point

CAPT. BILL BAILEY

ED

AF 78 098

U.S. AIR FORCE

C0243

Exhaust nozzle

Fixed ventral fin, used for improving stability at high speed

Landing gear compartment hatch

Red ribbons are removed before flight

In flight, the main undercarriage retracts into the fuselage

# Kart

The first karts were built in the US over 40 years ago and were known as go-karts. They were powered by lawnmower engines and were raced around supermarket parking lots. When faster karts were built, the racing was moved to custom-built tracks, and the machines were called karts.

Kart racing takes place on full-size racetracks. The tracks can be nearly five miles (eight kilometers) long.

*The driver's seat is positioned to the side of the kart, helping to make room for the engine*

*Roll restraint*

*A small, extra wing on each side helps to keep the kart on the ground*

*A kart engine is similar to the engine used in a racing motorcycle*

*The tire is a smaller version of a race car's tire*

*The sidepod allows the air to flow easily along the side of the kart*

ANDERSON Racing Karts

## How fast?

The fastest karts can reach 62 mph (100 kph) in less than 2.5 seconds. No road car in the world can accelerate this fast! Karts have a maximum speed of over 150 mph (240 kph), and can go around tight and twisty corners faster than any other type of racing vehicle. As a result, karts can lap some circuits faster than 500cc Grand Prix motorcycles!

*The kart is 2 feet (60 centimeters) high (without the roll restraint)*

## A bumpy ride

Karts have no springs for suspension. The tubular-steel frame does bend and flex a little, and the air-filled tires help, but the driver still gets a very bumpy ride.

*The driver changes gear with this lever*

*The position of the rear wing can be changed to suit different tracks*

## Sleek bodywork

To help achieve very high speeds on full-size racetracks, karts are equipped with aerodynamic bodywork. Air pressure on the bodywork also helps by pushing the kart down onto the track.

*The washers are made of aluminum to help keep the kart as light as possible*

*Most of this bodywork is removed when the kart races on very short tracks*

# Rescue helicopter

A helicopter is ideal for rescuing people from a mountain, from the sea, or for collecting a casualty from a boat. It will hover above the spot where it is needed, and lower a winchman and medical bag. If necessary, the winchman can descend 245 feet (75 meters) on a steel cable, though most winch drops are shorter. The winchman then brings the casualty back up to the helicopter, by stretcher if necessary.

*Each of the five rotor blades is about 30 feet (9 meters) in length*

*In flight, the pilot changes the angle of the rotor blades to control direction*

*A dome covers the radar scanner*

*The helicopter's rotor blades can be folded if it is carried on a ship*

**Helping the search**
This helicopter is called a Sea King. It is well-equipped for search and rescue, with navigational aids which enable it to pinpoint a distress signal from a long way away. Night vision equipment also allows the crew to see distress flares from a greater distance than they might otherwise.

*An anti-collision light flashes white. It is switched to red as the helicopter approaches a rescue*

*Winch*

*UHF aerial*

*The small tail rotor blades stop the helicopter from spinning around*

ZE370

ROYAL AIR FORCE

RESCUE

←DANGER

*The helicopter's tail can be folded to the side when it is carried on a ship*

*Sliding winch door*

The helicopter can carry 17 people, including its crew of four. It carries two stretchers.

*Though it looks like a grab rail, this is actually an antenna*

*Flotation bags inflate if the helicopter has to make an emergency landing on water*

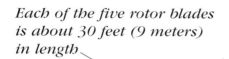

Observation window

The rotor blades spin to lift the helicopter into the air

The blades will become rigid when they spin

Sponson

Movable spotlight

The main wheels retract into the sponson in flight

The winch is worked by the winch operator, who uses a control panel just inside the open winch door.

Exhaust

The pilot and copilot sit in the cockpit, where they have dual controls

Floodlight

Movable spotlight

DANGER –

AREA

KEEP CLEAR

RELEASE-PRESS
BUTTON-TURN HANDLE
PULL OUT WINDOW

PULL TAB EXIT RELEASE

NO PUSH

RAF

RESCUE

E

Sponsons help to stabilize the helicopter if it lands on water

The hook is used for carrying loads

Door to nose compartment

These antennae home in on the radio signal from a casualty's boat

# Agricultural airplane

Some farmers spray their crops to prevent damage from pests or to fertilize the crops to help them grow. They may be growing corn, or peanuts, or cotton. A quick way of doing this is to use a plane: a type of aircraft known as a cropduster will swoop low over a field and spray a crop in minutes.

The white tip makes a white ring when the propeller spins, making it easier to see!

An unusual feature of this plane is that the propeller can be used to allow the plane to reverse when taxiing on the ground

The plane's single 750-horsepower engine is located behind the propeller

Engine exhaust

The propeller makes 2,000 revolutions (turns) each minute

Each wing is six foot (almost two meters) wide

Fuel is carried in the wings

Metal struts, known as boom hangars, support the spray boom

Air intake for engine

The landing gear is fixed and doesn't retract in flight

The pump that feeds the liquid product to the boom is turned by air flowing into this propeller

Air leaving the wings creates a downwash that forces the spray to cover both the top and the bottom of the crop's leaves.

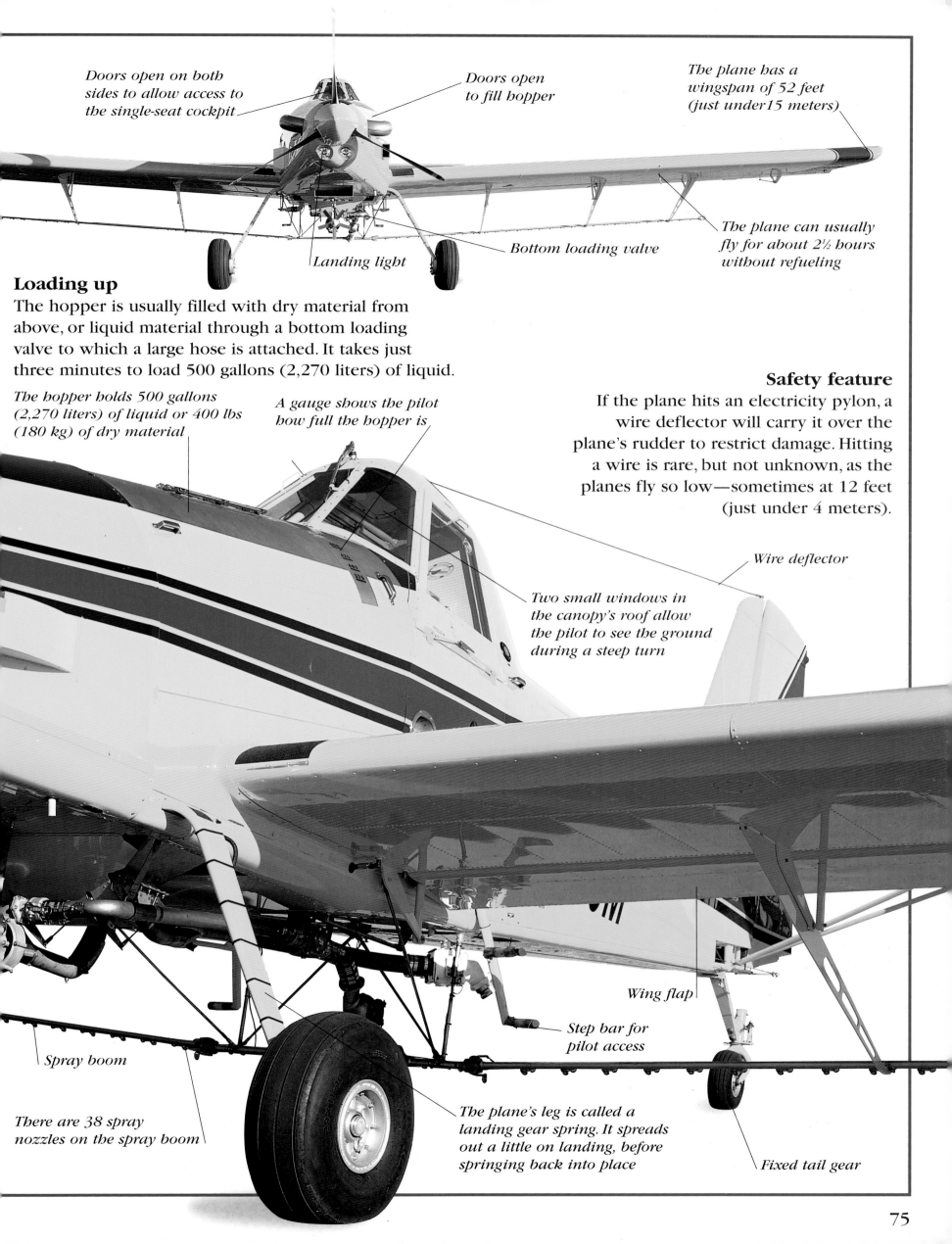

*Doors open on both sides to allow access to the single-seat cockpit*

*Doors open to fill hopper*

*The plane has a wingspan of 52 feet (just under 15 meters)*

*Landing light*

*Bottom loading valve*

*The plane can usually fly for about 2½ hours without refueling*

## Loading up

The hopper is usually filled with dry material from above, or liquid material through a bottom loading valve to which a large hose is attached. It takes just three minutes to load 500 gallons (2,270 liters) of liquid.

*The hopper holds 500 gallons (2,270 liters) of liquid or 400 lbs (180 kg) of dry material*

*A gauge shows the pilot how full the hopper is*

## Safety feature

If the plane hits an electricity pylon, a wire deflector will carry it over the plane's rudder to restrict damage. Hitting a wire is rare, but not unknown, as the planes fly so low—sometimes at 12 feet (just under 4 meters).

*Wire deflector*

*Two small windows in the canopy's roof allow the pilot to see the ground during a steep turn*

*Wing flap*

*Spray boom*

*Step bar for pilot access*

*There are 38 spray nozzles on the spray boom*

*The plane's leg is called a landing gear spring. It spreads out a little on landing, before springing back into place*

*Fixed tail gear*

# Endeavor

Take a close look at this strangely shaped truck. It has nowhere to attach a trailer, and its headlights and indicator lights aren't real—each one is a sticker. Look too at its radiator—it's not real either! In fact, the truck wouldn't be allowed on ordinary roads, but it's certainly not a toy truck. Its aerodynamic shape and low-to-ground body panels helped it to hurtle along at an incredible 226 mph (363 kph) to break a world speed record!

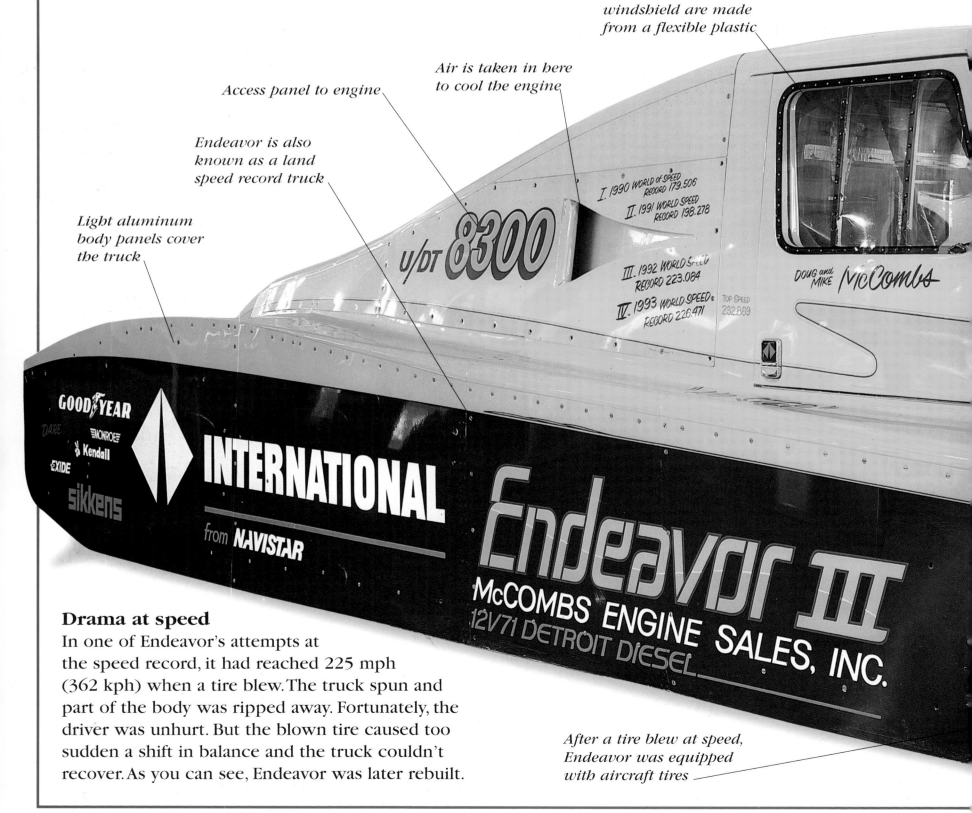

*Body panels cover two of the four wheels*

*The windows and windshield are made from a flexible plastic*

*Air is taken in here to cool the engine*

*Access panel to engine*

*Endeavor is also known as a land speed record truck*

*Light aluminum body panels cover the truck*

I. *1990 WORLD OF SPEED RECORD 179.506*
II. *1991 WORLD SPEED RECORD 198.278*
III. *1992 WORLD SPEED RECORD 223.084*
IV. *1993 WORLD SPEED RECORD 226.471* TOP SPEED 232.869

*Doug and Mike McCombs*

U/DT **8300**

GOOD**YEAR**
DARE MONROE Kendall
EXIDE
sikkens

**INTERNATIONAL**
*from* **NAVISTAR**

*Endeavor* **III**
McCOMBS ENGINE SALES, INC.
12V71 DETROIT DIESEL

## Drama at speed

In one of Endeavor's attempts at the speed record, it had reached 225 mph (362 kph) when a tire blew. The truck spun and part of the body was ripped away. Fortunately, the driver was unhurt. But the blown tire caused too sudden a shift in balance and the truck couldn't recover. As you can see, Endeavor was later rebuilt.

*After a tire blew at speed, Endeavor was equipped with aircraft tires*

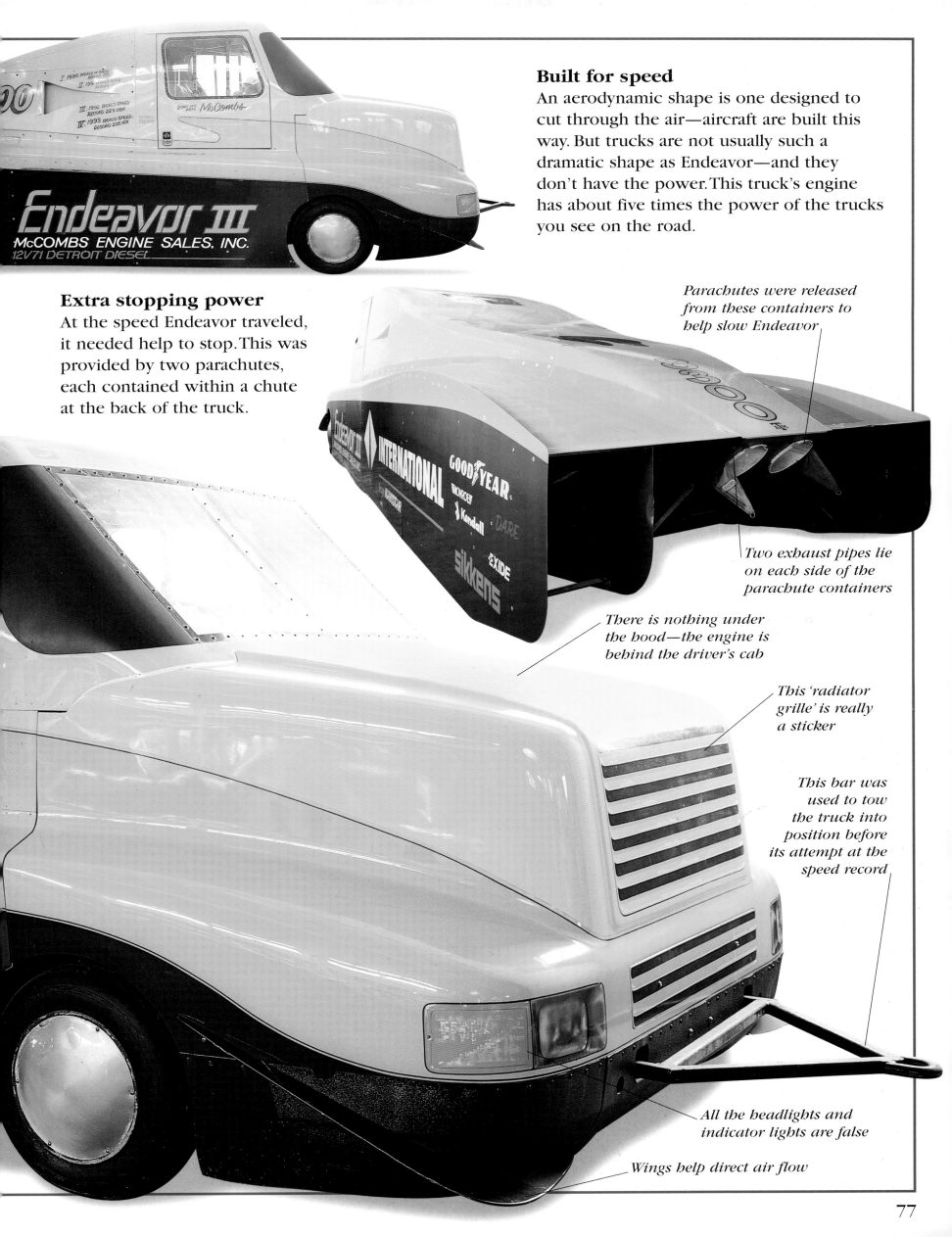

## Built for speed

An aerodynamic shape is one designed to cut through the air—aircraft are built this way. But trucks are not usually such a dramatic shape as Endeavor—and they don't have the power. This truck's engine has about five times the power of the trucks you see on the road.

## Extra stopping power

At the speed Endeavor traveled, it needed help to stop. This was provided by two parachutes, each contained within a chute at the back of the truck.

*Parachutes were released from these containers to help slow Endeavor*

*Two exhaust pipes lie on each side of the parachute containers*

*There is nothing under the hood—the engine is behind the driver's cab*

*This 'radiator grille' is really a sticker*

*This bar was used to tow the truck into position before its attempt at the speed record*

*All the headlights and indicator lights are false*

*Wings help direct air flow*

# Enduro bike

Enduro racing can take place through forests or across deserts. The races can take just a few hours, or last for days. Some races even take weeks to complete! For the longer races, the riders have support teams to help them take care of their bikes. At the end of each day, the race is stopped, and the teams set up camp for the night. Then the race starts again the following morning.

## Special bikes

Although enduro bikes look like some road bikes, they are very different. To survive day after day on the tough courses, the bikes have to be very strong. They also need to be able to go through sand, water, or mud without being damaged. To help achieve this, all top enduro bikes are carefully built by hand.

*Enduro bikes only look this clean before the race starts!*

## Riding high

All enduro bikes are built so that the engine is high off the ground. This enables the engine to clear obstacles, such as rocks and fallen trees.

*The plastic guard protects the rider's hand*

*A comfortable seat is important for very long races*

*The fuel tank is made of plastic to help keep the bike as light as possible*

*The high mudguard stops mud from clogging the front wheel*

*Gaiters stop the forks from being damaged by dust or mud*

An extra steel tube gives greater protection to the engine

This guard stops the rider's hands or feet from being caught in the chain if there is a crash

Ridden at high speed, the bikes take off into the air whenever they come to a small hill. This is very tiring for the riders, and only those in top shape can complete the long enduro races.

The front brake is small because a large brake could cause the tire to skid on loose surfaces

Each thin steel spoke may look weak, but is in fact very strong

The tires are often filled with a jellylike substance. This helps to prevent punctures

Long forks are needed to absorb the shocks when landing from big jumps

# Sports car

Sports car races usually last for a very long time. The most famous of them all takes place at Le Mans, in France, and lasts for 24 hours. Each car in this race has a team of two or three drivers to share the driving. Between the start and the finish, the winning car will travel around 3,100 miles (5,000 kilometers) —the distance from England to the US!

Whether it is day, night, dusk, or dawn, the drivers must drive as fast as they can. They must also drive carefully to make sure the car survives to the finish!

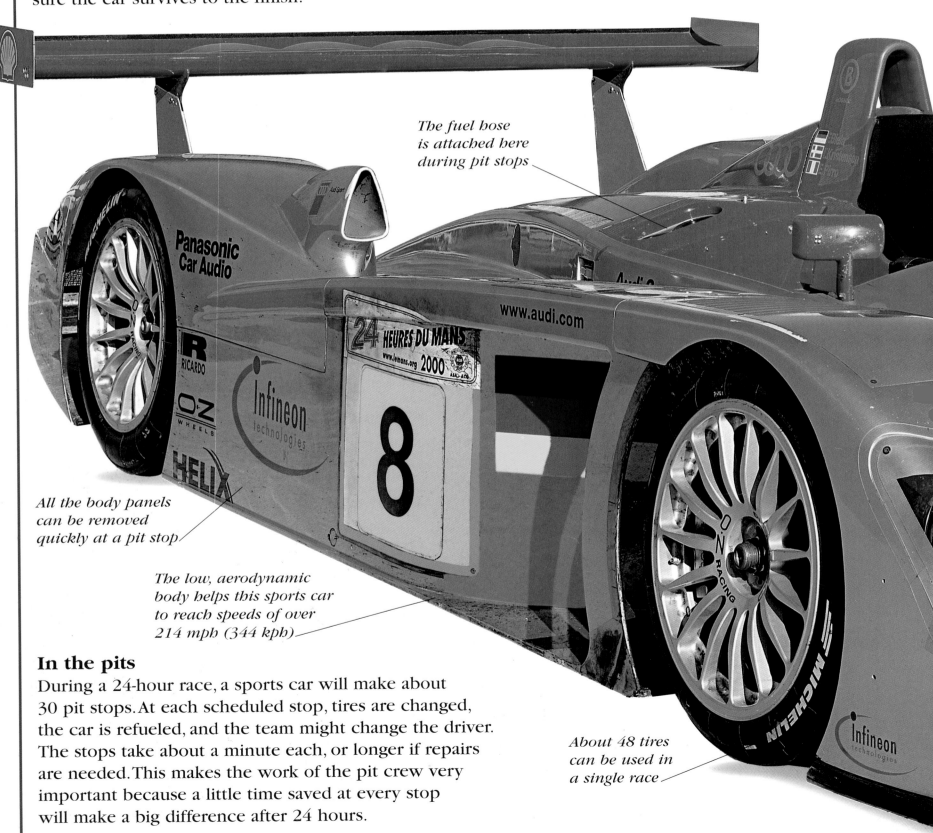

The fuel hose is attached here during pit stops

All the body panels can be removed quickly at a pit stop

The low, aerodynamic body helps this sports car to reach speeds of over 214 mph (344 kph)

About 48 tires can be used in a single race

## In the pits

During a 24-hour race, a sports car will make about 30 pit stops. At each scheduled stop, tires are changed, the car is refueled, and the team might change the driver. The stops take about a minute each, or longer if repairs are needed. This makes the work of the pit crew very important because a little time saved at every stop will make a big difference after 24 hours.

## Team colors

Many teams run more than one car in a race, and it is important that the cars can be easily identified. The Audi team's cars are all silver, but the red parts on this car are painted different colors on the other cars, so that the cars are easy to identify.

*When the car is moving, air enters here to help cool the engine and brakes*

*The small shield helps to deflect the air over the driver's head*

## Room for two

Unlike Formula One or CART cars, the driver of a sports car does not sit in the middle of the car. This is because the rules state that there must be room for a passenger seat.

*Powerful headlights are essential for nighttime racing*

*A towing eye enables the car to be taken away if it breaks down or crashes*

# Kit airplane

Imagine buying a kit and building your own airplane in a large garage! You could put together a plane like the Velocity, an eye-catching four-seater that looks very different than most light aircraft in the skies today.

*The winglet helps lift the aircraft and acts as a vertical stabilizer*

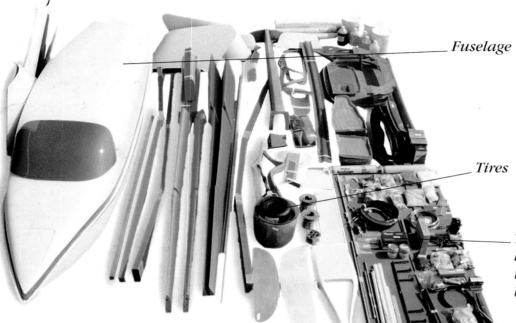

*Fuselage*

*Tires*

*The single gull-wing door opens upward*

*The build-a-plane kits come with all the necessary nuts, bolts, and screws*

## One big jig-saw puzzle
This Velocity kit takes about 1,200 hours to build. That's the same as working a five-day week for 34 weeks.

*Pitot tube*

*Step to aid access to cabin*

*The fiberglass body is so light that an adult can lift the nose off the ground*

*Small wings at the front, called canards, help to lift the aircraft*

*The plane seats four people including the pilot. It can carry about 600 lbs (272 kg) in weight of passengers and luggage*

## Why is it white?
Under the fiberglass surface is a lightweight core material that shrinks in excessive heat. A white surface doesn't absorb as much heat as a dark surface, which means that the core material is not as likely to get so hot that it shrinks.

*Nose wheel*

VELOCI

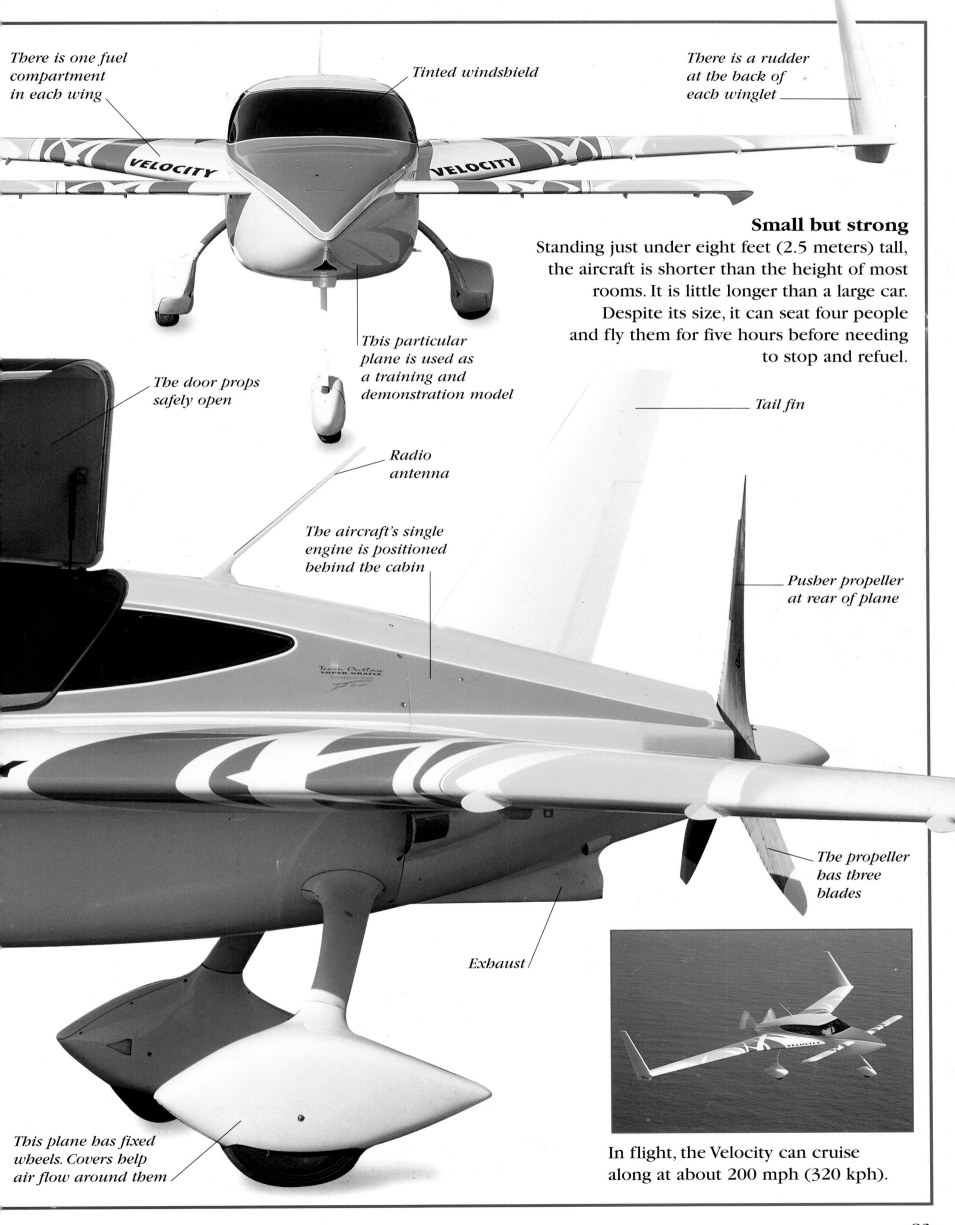

There is one fuel compartment in each wing

Tinted windshield

There is a rudder at the back of each winglet

**Small but strong**

Standing just under eight feet (2.5 meters) tall, the aircraft is shorter than the height of most rooms. It is little longer than a large car. Despite its size, it can seat four people and fly them for five hours before needing to stop and refuel.

This particular plane is used as a training and demonstration model

The door props safely open

Tail fin

Radio antenna

The aircraft's single engine is positioned behind the cabin

Pusher propeller at rear of plane

The propeller has three blades

Exhaust

This plane has fixed wheels. Covers help air flow around them

In flight, the Velocity can cruise along at about 200 mph (320 kph).

83

# American steam locomotives

The first railroad built across the United States was finished in May 1869. Colorful steam locomotives, like the ones shown here, carried settlers traveling to the new towns in the west. These locomotives were called 4-4-0s, because they had four driving wheels and four bogie wheels to guide the engine on the sometimes poor track. The bogie could swivel from side to side around the twisting tracks.

*The chimney let out smoke and used steam.*

*A large, powerful oil lamp warned people that a train was coming at night.*

*Door into the smoke box*

*The cowcatcher was a strong, metal grid for pushing wandering buffalo off the track.*

**Wood-burning locomotive**
*Jupiter* was an early American locomotive that burned wood for fuel. This famous engine worked on the Central Pacific Railroad. It had a large funnel-shaped chimney to catch the shower of sparks that came out of the engine with the smoke and steam.

## Coal-burning locomotive

By 1875, some American steam locomotives were using coal for fuel. This model shows how much of the pipework was on the outside for easy maintenance.

Tender

Warning bell

Four driving wheels

Four-wheeled bogie

Cowcatcher

The sand box sprinkled sand onto wet rails to give the wheels more grip.

The steam whistle used to warn people and animals of the train's approach.

The boiler turned the water into steam.

The firebox burned the coal to heat the water.

## Heading out west

*Locomotive 119* traveled westward across America on the Union Pacific Railroad. The engine weighed 40 tons (36 tonnes) and could pull about six passenger cars. At full steam, it could speed along at 50 miles (80 kilometers) per hour.

A large cab protected the driver and fireman from the wind and weather.

The tender carried 5 tons (4 tonnes) of coal and 2,400 gallons (9,000 liters) of water to power the train for 93 miles (150 kilometers).

The steam pushed the piston, which moved the connecting rod and turned the wheels.

# All-weather lifeboat

The emergency call or "shout" comes in and the six-person crew of the all-weather lifeboat drop whatever they are doing and rush to board the boat. They cast off and are then briefed on who is in trouble at sea. The lifeboat will head out in stormy seas, and can carry up to 78 survivors back to shore!

There are two steering positions. One is in the main cabin and the other is outside on the top deck.

## Power pack

The lifeboat is equipped with two engines, each the length of a small car. They are the same as the engines used to drive large, earth-moving trucks; in fact, the combined power would equal that of more than 1,000 horses! Together, the engines gulp about 50 gallons (230 liters) of diesel fuel per hour.

*A small inflatable rescue boat is carried on the top deck*

*This "A-frame" is used to hoist people out of the water*

*Emergency inflatable life raft*

*Each of the two life buoys is equipped with lights that float*

*The stern is the back of a boat*

Lifeboats
Royal National Lifeboat Institution

RNLB THE DUKE

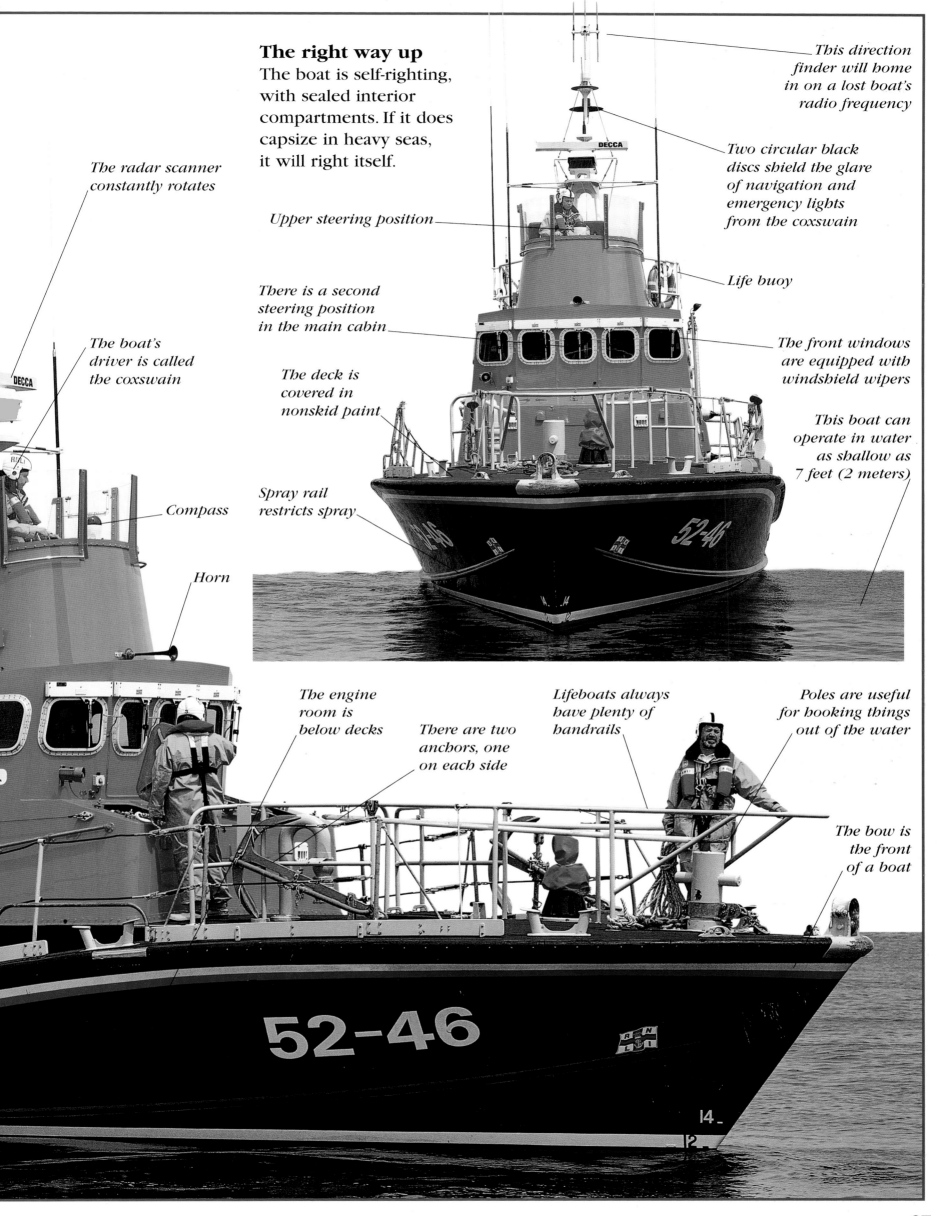

**The right way up**
The boat is self-righting, with sealed interior compartments. If it does capsize in heavy seas, it will right itself.

This direction finder will home in on a lost boat's radio frequency

The radar scanner constantly rotates

Two circular black discs shield the glare of navigation and emergency lights from the coxswain

Upper steering position

Life buoy

The boat's driver is called the coxswain

There is a second steering position in the main cabin

The front windows are equipped with windshield wipers

Compass

The deck is covered in nonskid paint

This boat can operate in water as shallow as 7 feet (2 meters)

Horn

Spray rail restricts spray

The engine room is below decks

Lifeboats always have plenty of handrails

Poles are useful for hooking things out of the water

There are two anchors, one on each side

The bow is the front of a boat

# Thrust

Two Thrust cars have held the Land Speed Record. But when ThrustSSC (SuperSonic Car) became the fastest car ever on October 15th, 1997, at a speed of more than 763 mph (1,228 kph), it also broke the sound barrier—the first car ever to do so.

**Breaking the sound barrier**

Try to imagine this: ThrustSSC is driving toward you, but you can't hear it until after it has gone past. This is because the car is traveling faster than the sound it is making—i.e., faster than the speed of sound! But attempting to break the sound barrier in a car was potentially very dangerous—no one knew how a car would behave at such high speeds.

*The driver sits between the engines.*

**ThrustSSC**

ThrustSSC is powered by two Rolls-Royce Spey jet engines, which together are three times as powerful as the single engine used in Thrust 2.

*The rear wing helps to keep the car stable at the speed of sound.*

*Hot air leaving the jet engine at very high speed pushes the car along.*

*The two large engines don't leave enough room to allow the front wheels to steer the car; so ThrustSSC is steered by a single rear wheel.*

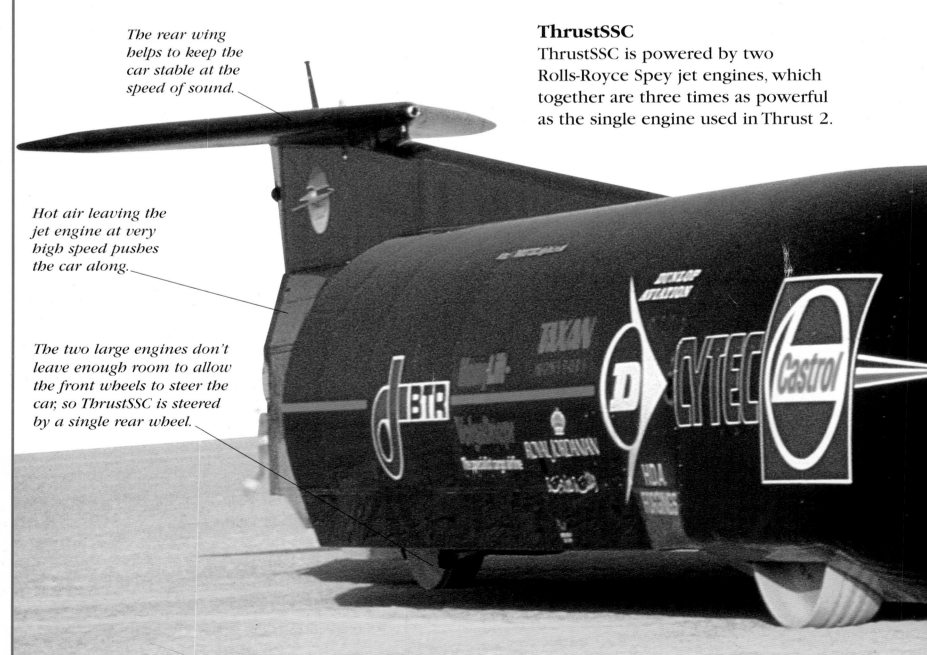

## Thrust 2

The British driver of Thrust 2, Richard Noble, took the land speed record from American Gary Gabelich. Thrust 2 held the Land Speed Record for 14 years at 633 mph (1,018 kph). Noble then went on to build ThrustSSC.

*The driver sits to one side of the central jet engine.*

*Sponsors' advertising helps pay for expensive record-breaking!*

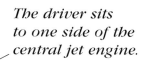

*The wheels are made of solid aluminum so they do not explode or disintegrate at very high speed.*

## Thrust team

A project to set the Land Speed Record and to be the first to break the sound barrier takes years of planning and preparation. It also takes an enormous amount of money and a large team of dedicated, talented, and hard-working people. From driver Andy Green, a pilot with Britain's Royal Air Force, to the designers, engineers, cooks, and accountants—every member of the team had a very important job.

*Air is sucked into the jet engine this end.*

*The very sharp nose cuts through the air easily.*

# Chinook helicopter

A helicopter can hover and pick up a load from a very restricted space. It might be lifting logs from a heavily wooded hillside or transporting huge pipes. This Chinook helicopter is unusually powerful. It has been stripped of unnecessary equipment to make it lighter so that it can lift more than its own weight in cargo. It is known as a utility Chinook.

*The blades spin around at 225 times per minute*

The hefty steel cable used to lift loads is one inch (2.5 cm) thick and 200 feet (60 meters) long.

*Each rotor blade is 30 feet (nine meters) in length*

## A thirst for fuel

Helicopter engines burn up a lot of fuel spinning the rotors to lift the machine up. During routine heavy-lift operations, this Chinook uses 333 gallons (1,515 liters) of fuel per hour. It is typically refueled every 1½ hours.

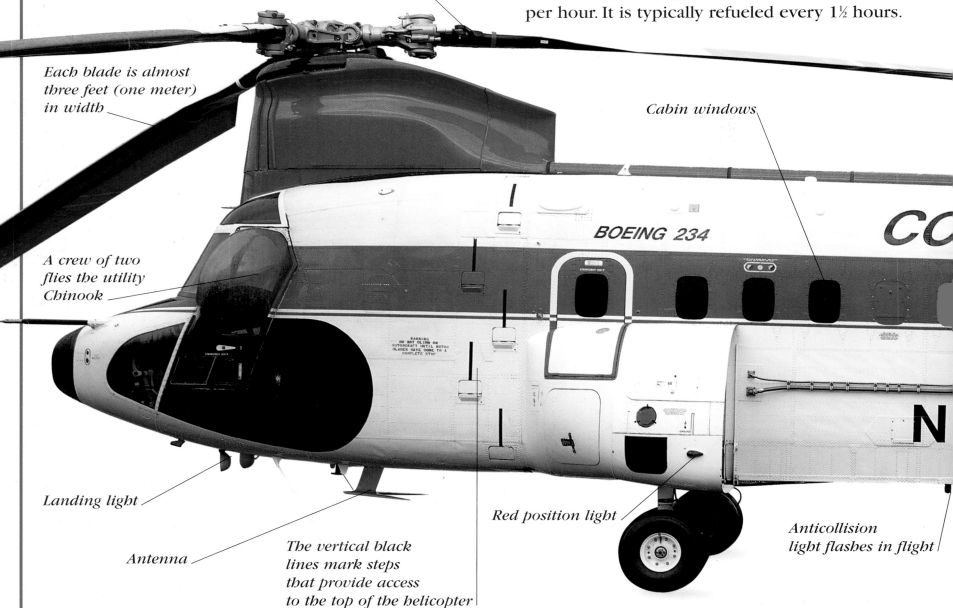

*Each blade is almost three feet (one meter) in width*

*Cabin windows*

*A crew of two flies the utility Chinook*

BOEING 234

CO

N

*Landing light*

*Antenna*

*The vertical black lines mark steps that provide access to the top of the helicopter*

*Red position light*

*Anticollision light flashes in flight*

## Flight control

A pilot works with a copilot, so the cockpit controls are the same on both sides. Both pilot and copilot have more than 150 control buttons and switches around them.

*The blades droop when the Chinook is on the ground*

*Bubble windows provide the pilot with excellent visibility of the load below*

*It is a US Forest Service requirement that the tops of the blades are yellow and white*

The inside is empty of seats to keep weight low. A car could fit into the space left behind.

*There are almost 80,000 moving parts on the helicopter*

*The fore and aft rotor blades interweave as they spin to lift the helicopter into the air*

*One of two turbine engines*

*A screen stops small things from hitting the engine*

*Emergency exit door*

*Fuel line to pump fuel to engines*

*External cargo hook*

*Steerable landing gear*

*A military Chinook has a rear cargo access ramp, but this has been removed from the utility Chinook as it is unnecessary and would add unwanted weight*

# Trial truck

Climb into this truck, strap on your five-point safety harness, and hold on tight as the driver maneuvers about 250 ft (75 m) down an almost vertical slope and surges on through 6 ft (2 m) of muddy water. The truck competes in European truck trials over rough ground, and the driver's job is to keep it moving without rolling the truck or hitting marker posts.

*The trial truck can climb steep hills.*

*A steel roll bar will protect the occupants if the truck rolls over*

*Air to cool the engine can be taken in through a pipe on top of the driver's cab so the truck can drive through water*

*There are two circular access openings in the roof of the cab*

*Tow eye*

*This truck was originally designed to push a bulldozer blade. The blade attached here*

## More air?

A tire's air pressure determines how hard it is: the firmer the ground, the harder the tire needs to be. This truck's eight tires can be individually inflated or deflated from the driver's seat; so as the ground gets muddier, air can be let out to make the tire softer.

*The safety roll bar runs through the inside of the cab*

*A unique race number identifies each truck*

*Spotlight*

*This lever will shut down power in an emergency*

*The 40-gallon (180-liter) fuel tank is in the back, where it avoids damage from rough ground*

*The driver and navigator wear helmets and maintain radio contact*

*This button will stop the engine*

*This metal plate hides a hole for the winch cable*

*Covers protect the headlights from breaking; they are not required for racing*

## Heavy accessories

A spare tire is kept in the trailer. Weighing almost a quarter of a ton, the tire is so heavy it has to be lifted out with a crane that is permanently fixed to the back of the truck.

*A recovery winch is located underneath the cargo bed. Its steel cable can feed out through the front or back of the truck*

*This 11.5-ft (3.5-m)-long rigid tow bar hooks onto the front of the cab if required*

# Lamborghini

The Italian tractor manufacturer Lamborghini started making cars less than fifty years ago. Their cars have always been fast and spectacular. Lamborghinis are extremely complex—made out of incredibly expensive materials and parts. They are built so slowly and carefully that the factory only makes three cars a day, which explains why Lamborghinis are so rare and expensive.

## Lamborghini Diablo

The Lamborghini Diablo is one of the world's most exotic, and expensive, sports cars. It is a supercar for the super-rich with a top speed of more than 206 mph (330 kph).

*An unusual feature, which is also used on other Lamborghinis, is the vertically opening doors.*

*The engine is in the back, leaving no room for rear seats.*

*Luxurious leather seats*

*The large wheels are similar to those used on racing cars.*

## Top-notch

The Diablo can reach high speeds because of its advanced and powerful engine and its exceptionally aerodynamic body shape.

The large rear wing helps keep the car stable at 206 mph (330 kph).

The powerful 1.5-gallon (5.7-liter) engine can accelerate the Diablo from standstill to 60 mph (100 kph) in under four seconds.

## Careful reversing!

The reverse gear on the Diablo is for parking and turning the car around, just like on other cars. But drivers should take special care when backing the Diablo into a small parking space—the car will do more than 60 mph (100 kph) in reverse!

The Diablo is available with an open top or a fixed roof.

The Lamborghini emblem—a bull on a black background—can also be found on the company's tractors.

The ground clearance at the front can be adjusted by the driver.

# Index